GW01090577

NEW LANGUAGE LESSONS

LEAVING CERTIFICATE ENGLISH
PAPER 1
HIGHER LEVEL

MARTIN KIERAN & FRANCES ROCKS

Gill Education

Hume Avenue

Park West

Dublin 12

www.gilleducation.ie

Gill Education is an imprint of M.H. Gill & Co.

© Martin Kieran and Frances Rocks 2024

ISBN: 978-0-7171-99457

All rights reserved. No part of this publication may be copied,
reproduced or transmitted in any form or by any means without
written permission of the publishers or else under the terms of
any licence permitting limited copying issued by the Irish Copyright
Licensing Agency.

Design: Sarah McCoy

Print origination: Carole Lynch

At the time of going to press, all web addresses were active and
contained information relevant to the topics in this book. Gill Education
does not, however, accept responsibility for the content or views contained
on these websites. Content, views and addresses may change beyond
the publisher or author's control. Students should always be supervised
when reviewing websites.

For permission to reproduce photographs, the authors and publisher
gratefully acknowledge the following:

© Adobe Stock: IV, 3, 5, 7, 16, 25, 26, 33, 35, 36, 37, 38, 41, 46, 48, 53, 60,
64, 73, 80, 79, 85, 96, 103, 104, 105, 120, 123, 130, 132, 135, 136, 141, 146,
156, 160, 167, 168, 170, 175, 178, 182; © Alamy: 13B, 18, 19, 21, 23, 39BR, 42,
43, 45, 56, 57, 58, 74, 87, 90T, 100, 101, 118, 125, 134RT, 137B, 143, 180;
© iStock/Getty Premium: VI, 9, 10, 12, 13T, 14, 28, 30, 39T, 39BL, 40, 50, 51, 59,
63, 65, 67, 69, 71, 75, 76, 78, 81, 83, 84, 88, 90B, 93, 99, 108, 109, 112, 115,
116, 127, 128, 129, 134L, 134RB, 137T, 138, 139, 145, 148, 150, 152, 153, 155,
157, 162, 164, 165, 181; © Shutterstock: 53T.

The authors and publisher have made every effort to trace all copyright
holders. If, however, any have been inadvertently overlooked, we would be
pleased to make the necessary arrangement at the first opportunity.

PEFC Certified
This product is from
sustainably managed
forests and controlled
sources
PEFC
PEFC/14-38-00260   www.pefc.co.uk

Table of Contents

Introduction   **v**

Genres of Language   **vi**

Comprehending A Overview   2

Lesson 1:	Narrative and Aesthetic Writing	3
Lesson 2:	Descriptive Writing	7
Lesson 3:	Writing Personal Responses	9
Lesson 4:	Gothic Writing	13
Lesson 5:	Analysing Setting	17
Lesson 6:	Analysing a Writer's Style	20
Lesson 7:	Crime Writing	24
Lesson 8:	Travel Writing	28
Lesson 9:	Responding to Informative Texts	33
Lesson 10:	Visual Literacy	37
Lesson 11:	Autobiographical Writing	42
Lesson 12:	Comprehending A – Practice Text	46

Comprehending B Overview   49

Lesson 13:	Writing a Short Talk	50
Lesson 14:	Writing Reviews	54
Lesson 15:	Short Articles	58
Lesson 16:	Writing Effective Articles	62
Lesson 17:	Opinion Pieces	66
Lesson 18:	Podcasts	70
Lesson 19:	Writing a Short Speech	74
Lesson 20:	Formal Emails	79
Lesson 21:	Personal Journals and Diaries	84
Lesson 22:	Blogs	89
Lesson 23:	Writing an Introduction	95
Lesson 24:	Open Letters	100

Composing Overview 106

Lesson 25: Personal Essays 108

Lesson 26: Personal Essay-Writing Skills 113

Lesson 27: Writing Effective Personal Essays 116

Lesson 28: Writing Effective Feature Articles 120

Lesson 29: Discursive Writing 126

Lesson 30: Effective Discursive Essays 130

Lesson 31: Using Descriptive Language 135

Lesson 32: Effective Descriptive Essays 138

Lesson 33: The Language of Information 142

Lesson 34: Speech-Writing 147

Lesson 35: Effective Persuasive Essays 151

Lesson 36: Introduction to Short Story Writing 156

Lesson 37: Sample Story 1 161

Lesson 38: Sample Story 2 166

Lesson 39: Sample Story 3 171

Lesson 40: Mechanics – Grammar and Spelling 179

Acknowledgements Inside back cover

Introduction

OVERVIEW

Leaving Certificate English Paper 1 **focuses on key skills** of understanding, remembering, analysing, evaluating and creating.

It aims at developing the student's ability to:

- Express critical viewpoints
- Question the authority of texts
- Compare and contrast a range of texts

'READING' EXAMINATION QUESTIONS

In the examination, it's important to **study the wording of questions** closely before you begin writing responses. **Highlight the important 'command words'** in the question, so that you are clear about the task.

- **Analyse:** Consider and question closely in order to explain.
- **Comment on:** Respond critically to subject matter and/or style of writing.
- **Compare and contrast:** Examine similarities and differences.
- **Define:** Explain exactly what something means.
- **Develop your point of view:** Support the points you make through further discussion.
- **Discuss:** Examine and distinguish positive and negative points.
- **Evaluate:** Consider something carefully, explaining how significant or important it is.
- **Explain:** Clarify by giving details and/or reasons.
- **Identify:** Find examples.
- **Illustrate:** Give more information or examples to explain or prove something.
- **Outline:** Briefly describe main points.

Genres of Language

To prepare for Leaving Certificate Higher Level English, you are expected to be familiar with the five main genres (types) of language on the examination paper.

1. INFORMATIVE WRITING

Found in newspapers, reports, etc.

- ✔ Factual, direct, using verifiable data
- ✔ Clearly organised, accessible language

2. ARGUMENTATIVE WRITING

Found in newspapers, discussions, etc.

- ✔ Discursive and balanced, using valid evidence
- ✔ Reasonable, rational language

3. PERSUASIVE WRITING

Found in speeches, opinion pieces, debates, etc.

- ✔ Presents a strong view or opinion
- ✔ Emphatic, often emotional language

4. NARRATIVE WRITING

Found in novels, plays, films, etc.

- ✔ Story-telling based on plot, characterisation and conflict
- ✔ Associated with fiction and personal writing

5. AESTHETIC WRITING

Found in short stories, poetry, diaries, etc.

- ✔ Appeals to our appreciation of beauty
- ✔ Poetic imaginative language, often using rich imagery

NOTE

'The general functions of language outlined here will continually mix and mingle within texts and genres. So, there can be an aesthetic argument, a persuasive narrative, or an informative play.'

Department of Education English Syllabus

COMPREHENDING A SECTION

In Leaving Certificate Higher Level English, the **Comprehending A** section is worth 50 marks and has three questions:

(i) and **(ii)** are each worth 15 marks; **(iii)** is worth 20 marks.

COMPREHENDING B AND COMPOSING SECTIONS

Both the Comprehending B and Composing sections are marked using the PCLM marking system.

This refers to: **P**urpose, **C**oherence, **L**anguage and **M**echanics.

NOTE

The composition assignments are intended to reflect language study in the areas of information, argument, persuasion, narration and the aesthetic use of language.

PCLM MARKING SCHEME

Purpose: Are all aspects of the question being addressed? **(30% of the marks)**

Coherence: Is the response controlled, paragraphed and sustained? **(30% of the marks)**

Language: How appropriate is the writing with regard to expression, vocabulary, freshness, fluency and punctuation? **(30% of the marks)**

Mechanics: Are spellings and grammar accurate? **(10% of the marks)**

NOTE

See further details of how the PCLM marking scheme is applied by examiners in the Comprehending B Overview (p. 49) and Composing Overview (p. 106).

COMPREHENDING A OVERVIEW

Comprehending A questions test your ability to read, understand, analyse and respond to a particular text. This question is worth **50 marks** and has three parts.

COMPREHENDING A PART (I)

Comprehending A Part (i) deals with the **content** (subject matter) of the text. It is often referred to as an 'information retrieval' question and is worth **15 marks**.

You might be asked to outline in your own words:

- Your **observations** about a character, relationship, viewpoint or ideas in the text.
- The **impressions** you get of particular places, atmospheres, ideas, etc.
- **Insights** you gained into a subject or the writer's own views, lifestyle, etc.

Three short paragraphs, based on three relevant points, should be sufficient. Aim for around **230 words**.

COMPREHENDING A PART (II)

This question, also worth **15 marks**, usually asks candidates to **respond personally** to the text. You might be asked to consider certain events, ideas, opinions, etc. mentioned in the extract. Again, aim for around **230 words**.

COMPREHENDING A PART (III)

Comprehending A Part (iii) focuses on the **writing style** and is worth **20 marks**. You will usually be asked to discuss **key features of language** used in the text:

- Identify **elements of style** – narrative, descriptive, persuasive, informative, etc.
- Discuss the **impact** of particular stylistic features.
- Explain **how the writer creates setting, mood, conflict, atmosphere, etc.**
- Examine the **effect of any visual images**.
- Comment on the **extent** to which the writing is interesting, engaging, entertaining, informative, dramatic, etc.

Four short paragraphs, based on four relevant points, should be sufficient. Aim to write around **300 words**.

NOTE

See further details of how the Comprehending A marking scheme is applied by examiners in the introduction (p. vii).

Narrative and Aesthetic Writing

SNOWFLAKE

This text is taken from Louise Nealon's novel, *Snowflake*. It tells the story of Debbie, a young girl who lives on a dairy farm in Kildare and is good friends with her uncle.

Read the following extract carefully, paying particular attention to the narrative style.

My uncle Billy lives in a caravan in a field at the back of my house. The first time I saw another caravan on the road I thought that someone – another child – had kidnapped him on me. It was only then that I learned caravans were meant to move. Billy's caravan never went anywhere. It was plonked[1] on a bed of concrete blocks, right beside me from the day I was born.

I used to visit Billy at night when I was too afraid to go to sleep. Billy said that I was only allowed out of the house if I could see the moon from my window and if I brought him wishes[2] from the garden. On the night of my eighth birthday, the sight of a round, fat moon sent me straight down the stairs and out the back door, the wet grass on my bare feet, the thorns of the hedge grabbing me, pulling me back by the sleeves of my pyjamas.

I knew where the wishes hung out. A coven[3] of them grew close to the caravan on the other side of the hedge. I picked them one by one, satisfied by the soft snap of stem and sticky juice of severed end, the bump of one fluffy white head into another. I cupped my hand around them as though protecting candles from the wind, careful not to knock off a single wisp of wish and lose it to the night.

I twirled the syllables around my head as I collected them – dandelion, dandelion, dandelion. Earlier that day, we had looked up the word in the big dictionary underneath Billy's bed. He explained that it came from the French term – dents de lion – lion's teeth. The dandelion began as a pretty thing and the petals of its skirt were pointy and yellow like a tutu.[4]

'This is its daytime dress but the flower eventually needs to go to sleep. It withers and looks tired and haggard and just when you think it's time is up' – Billy held up his fist – 'it turns into a clock.' He uncurled his fingers and produced a white candy-floss dandelion from behind his back. 'A puff-ball moon. A holy communion of wishes.' He let me blow the wishes away like birthday candles. 'A constellation[5] of dreams.'

Billy marvelled at the bouquet of wishes I presented to him when he opened the caravan door. I picked as many as I could find to impress him.

'I knew it,' he said. 'I just knew that the moon would come out for your birthday.'

We filled an empty jam jar with water and blew the cottony heads of the dandelions into it, their feathers floating on the meniscus[6] like tiny swimmers lying on their backs. I closed the lid on the jar and shook the wishes, celebrating them, watching them dance. We left the jar on top of a dank stack of newspapers to stare out of the caravan's plastic window.

Billy heated a saucepan of milk on the hob of his gas cooker. His kitchen looked like a toy I hoped to get for Christmas. It always surprised me when it worked in real life. He let me stir the milk until it bubbled and formed little white sheets of skin that I pulled away with the back of a spoon. He poured in the chocolate powder and I whisked the spoon around and around until my arm hurt. We tipped the steaming brown stream into a flask and brought it up to the roof to watch the stars.

It took days for the dandelion seeds to fully submerge in the jar. They clung to the surface, hanging from their ceiling of water until it seemed like they either gave up or got bored. Just when the world thought they were goners, tiny little green shoots appeared like plant mermaids growing tails underwater. Billy called me to come over and marvel at the stubborn little yokes,[7] the wishes that refused to die.

Today is my eighteenth birthday. I'm a bit nervous knocking on Billy's door. I don't really visit him at night anymore. The outside of the caravan is cold against my knuckles. It has a lining of rubber along the sides like a fridge door. I dig my nails into the squishiness and tear a bit away. It comes off in a smooth strip like a sliver of fat off a ham. There is a shuffle of papers and the squeeze of steps across the floor. Billy opens the door and tries his best not to seem surprised to see me.

'Well,' he says, making his way back to his armchair.

'Sleeping Beauty,' I greet him. He didn't get up for milking this morning and I had to do it for him.

'Yeah, sorry about that.'

'On my birthday and all,' I say.

1. placed
2. dandelion puff-balls
3. group
4. ballet dress
5. pattern
6. surface
7. things

LANGUAGE OF NARRATION – STYLISTIC FEATURES

- ○ Narrative voice
- ○ Characterisation
- ○ Tension and conflict
- ○ Setting
- ○ Plot
- ○ Atmosphere
- ○ Dialogue
- ○ Vivid description

AESTHETIC WRITING

- Aesthetic writing refers to language that appeals to our sense of beauty. It is closely associated with an imaginative and carefully crafted lyrical style.
- While usually evident in poetry and fiction, aesthetic language may also be found in personal and descriptive writing.
- Think of the literary terms you learnt for your poetry studies when you are thinking about a writer's aesthetic style.
- Common features of aesthetic language include vivid imagery, evocative tones, lively comparisons, sound effects and rhythm.

WORD POWER

Close analysis of language use in the text is essential for answering questions successfully. The following discussion notes focus on key words and phrases that illustrate the writer's **effective narrative skill**.

- Debbie's engaging **narrative voice** invites readers into a world of imagination and discovery. Her vibrant personality is evident in her enthusiastic adventures – climbing up on the caravan roof 'to watch the stars'.

- **Descriptive details** show her innocent experience of nature ('a round fat moon', 'wet grass on my bare feet').

- The close relationship between Debbie and her uncle is revealed in her **backstory** of their early conversations about dandelions and life's many mysteries.

- The beauty of the **rural setting** and Billy's cramped caravan add realism.

- **Aesthetic use of language** – personification ('thorns of the hedge grabbing me'), lively comparisons ('pointy and yellow like a tutu') and musical sound effects ('twirled the syllables') highlight Debbie's personal experiences.

- Vivid, sensual **imagery** gives a tactile quality to the narrative ('shoots appeared like plant mermaids growing tails under water').

- The **storyline develops** when Debbie returns to the present ('her eighteenth birthday'). Readers can recognise signs of how both she and Billy have changed – and that she now seems to be the stronger person in the relationship.

SAMPLE COMPREHENDING A QUESTION

QUESTION A

(iii) Features of both narrative and aesthetic writing are used effectively by Louise Nealon to convey Debbie's experiences of growing up in rural Ireland.

Discuss this statement, supporting your response with reference to four language features in the extract. You may include features of narrative writing, features of aesthetic writing, or both in your discussion.

(20)

SAMPLE ANSWER

1. In this extract, the central character is interesting because we see her at two different stages in her life. The writer uses the narrative technique of flashback to show what Debbie's childhood was like. I got the impression of a typical eight-year-old with an active imagination. She is fascinated by dandelions because her uncle makes up stories about them. I think a good novel has characters that we can relate to and Debbie is very likeable.

> First stylistic feature – narrative technique of flashback
>
> Effect – engages sympathy for Debbie

2. Billy is a role model for Debbie. She loves bringing him the dandelions, 'I picked as any as I could find to impress him'. Any reader would like to know more about how their lives will turn out as Debbie moves on. There is a strong hint at the end that Billy is no longer able to cope and now depends on Debbie. This really involves the reader in wondering about how the story will work out.

> Second narrative technique of suspense
>
> Effect – engages the reader's curiosity

3. I thought Debbie's world was true to life for a young person growing up in the country. There is some detailed description of the dandelions and the night-time settings. These set the magical mood. Everything is new to the child – especially Billy's tales about making wishes by blowing the fluffy heads off dandelions. Debbie sees him as a sort of magician who can do tricks by producing 'a candy floss dandelion from behind his back'.

> Third feature – rich imaginative description
>
> Effect – creates a special mood

4. There is also some very poetic language in this extract. Debbie and her uncle live in a very quiet isolated area and there is a lot of love between them. They share a love for the simple lifestyle and speak naturally to each other. This is seen in all the descriptive images of the farm. Sounds really appeal to her – 'the soft snap of stem', 'squishiness'. The aesthetic writing brings her experiences to life and makes the story more enjoyable.

> Fourth feature – poetic/aesthetic language
>
> Effect – adds to the reader's pleasure

EXAMINER'S COMMENT

- Well-focused insightful comments on the effective use of narrative and aesthetic language.

- Interesting points about characters, setting, the magical mood and the lyrical writing.

- Although some of these might have been developed more, the answer showed a clear understanding of story-telling and the impact of a writer's style.

- Generally supportive quotations throughout, well integrated into the discussion.   **(20/20)**

CLASS/HOMEWORK ACTIVITY

QUESTION A

(i)   Based on your reading of the above extract from *Snowflake*, explain three insights you gain into the relationship between Debbie and her uncle. Support your answer with reference to the text.   **(15)**

 Allow about 15 minutes and aim to write three focused, supported points.

PROMPT

- What are your first impressions of the relationship?
- Why do you think Debbie and her uncle are so close?
- What do both characters have in common?
- How has their relationship changed over time?
- Is the relationship happy or sad? Or both?

NOTE

In Comprehending questions, an **insight** is usually something new that you became aware of when reading a text. Insights refer to deeper understandings or lessons that you gain.

Learning aim: To analyse and discuss key features of descriptive writing

- **Descriptive language** invites readers into the world of the story. They can imagine what characters, places or experiences are like.

- This heightens how readers engage with what is being described and their response to it.

KEY ELEMENTS OF DESCRIPTIVE WRITING

○ Vivid details ○ Precise language ○ Strong verbs ○ Colourful imagery ○ Comparison
○ Personification ○ Atmosphere ○ Focus on the senses (sight, hearing, smell, touch and taste)

THE HOME SCAR

This text is taken from Kathleen MacMahon's novel, *The Home Scar*, which begins with an account of the re-emergence of a 'drowned' forest on the Galway coastline during a 2014 storm.

Read the following extract carefully, paying particular attention to the writer's descriptive language use.

The storm came in late summer. It swept in off the Atlantic, bringing high seas and gale force winds that battered the whole of the west coast. It was severe enough to earn itself a name, a red warning, a lead slot on the news. People were told to stay away from the sea, but even so some ventured out to observe the spectacle. There were surfers seen riding the waves in Sligo, the occasional swimmer at Salthill. They were endangering the lives of others as well as their own, according to the spokesperson for Water Safety Ireland who went on the radio to warn of the risks. As it happened, there was nobody drowned, leading some to say the dangers had been exaggerated. The storm had not been so dramatic after all. Bearing in mind what was happening in the rest of the world, it seemed blessedly tame.

The TV was at that time broadcasting pictures on a nightly basis of forest fires in Catalonia. Vast tracts of the Amazon were in flames, while in Mexico there were reports of snow. A hellish heatwave raged across Europe, with record-breaking temperatures in France, Germany and Poland. City dwellers took to the fountains to cool down. Ice pops were handed out to the zoo animals.

In North America there was rain, so much of it that in New York City the subway stations flooded. Dive teams had to be called in to evacuate people from their homes in Illinois. There was hail the size of baseballs in Montana, a landslide in Ohio, cyclones[1] over the Atlantic. It was the tail end of one of those storms that had swept across Ireland, ripping the roofs off schools and football stadiums. Trees were uprooted, weather buoys[2] unmoored. But still, we were lucky, people said. It could have been worse.

In the days that followed, the army was called in to help clear the debris from the roads. Electricity repair crews worked night and day to restore power to thousands of homes. Loss adjustors[3] inspected the damage to property, while scientists lined up to blame global warming. Amid all this activity, one thing went unnoticed. It was happened upon purely by chance, by a man out walking his dog on the beach. The man wasn't quite sure what it was that he had found, but he at least had the wit to tell someone about it. Thus was the enormity of his discovery understood and eventually made public. What the storm had exposed was an ancient drowned forest.

The first newspaper to cover the story was the *Connacht Tribune*. A regional paper of long and distinguished standing, the *Tribune*'s newsroom was located in the city of Galway, and it was there that a young reporter took a call about the strange find. Glad of a chance to escape the office, the reporter drove the dozen miles out the coast road to the location described. The dog walker was waiting for him there, with barely contained excitement. It might have been a mutilated[4] body he'd found and not some dead trees. The reporter changed into his wellies, which he kept in the boot of his car, and together they trudged across a muddy field to the beach.

At first it wasn't much to see. The trees were no more than stumps, barely a foot high. The stumps stood knee-deep in the wet sand like a ghostly, decapitated army. It was only when you hunkered[5] down close to the sand that you were taken by the beauty of them. The grain of the wood was clearly visible, tiger-striped in some places, rounding into whorls[6] in others. The reporter had no knowledge of natural history, but he knew that he was in the presence of something marvellous.

1. **hurricanes**
2. **floats**
3. **insurance advisers**
4. **disfigured**
5. **crouched**
6. **coil shapes**

WORD POWER

Close analysis of language use in the text is essential for answering questions successfully. The following discussion notes focus on key words and phrases that illustrate **the writer's effective descriptive skill**.

- The extract begins with a powerful depiction of the storm. **Energetic verbs** ('swept', 'battered') reflect the intensity and violence of nature.

- Paragraphs two and three focus on reports of extraordinary weather conditions worldwide. **Precise details** illustrate the unusual 'record-breaking temperatures' across Europe.

- **Dynamic images** emphasise the destruction caused by the storm in Ireland: 'Trees were uprooted, weather buoys unmoored'.

- Paragraph four describes **the huge interest** among local people, following the discovery of 'an ancient drowned forest' by a dog walker who was 'barely able to conceal his excitement'.

- **Haunting language** evokes the desolate coastline, highlighting its surreal atmosphere. A striking simile, comparing the 'dead trees' to 'a ghostly, decapitated army', reflects the writer's fascination with this bleakly beautiful example of Ireland's natural history.

CLASS/HOMEWORK ACTIVITY

QUESTION A

(iii) Kathleen MacMahon's descriptive writing is rich in language and imagery. Discuss this statement, supporting your response with reference to four features of descriptive style evident in the above extract from *The Home Scar*. **(20)**

🕐 **Allow about 20 minutes and aim to write four focused, supported points.**
The Word Power notes on descriptive writing may be helpful in responding to the question.

PLANNING YOUR RESPONSE

In answering Comprehending A personal response questions, you will be expected to consider and **express your own ideas and feelings about aspects of a text.** The wording of questions can vary, for example:

- Give your personal response to the writer's claim that …

- To what extent can you relate the writer's observations to your own experience of …?

- Discuss the extent to which you agree or disagree with the view that …

EFFECTIVE PERSONAL RESPONSES WILL INCLUDE SOME OF THESE ELEMENTS:

- Evidence of **analysis** or critical thinking

- Well-supported reasonable **arguments** or observations

- Appropriate **anecdotes** from your own experience

- Relevant **links** to the extract

- **References** to other texts, media or information sources

- An honest, **confident approach** to expressing your opinions

- Clear, **accessible expression**; enthusiastic tone, etc.

DO TREES TALK TO EACH OTHER?

The following text explores whether or not trees can communicate. It was written by Richard Grant for the science section of a magazine.

Read the extract carefully, paying particular attention to the writer's views and ideas.

I'm walking in the Eiffel Mountains in western Germany, through cathedral-like groves of oak and beech, and there's a strange unmoored[1] feeling of entering a fairy tale. The trees have become vibrantly alive and charged with wonder. They're communicating with one another, for starters. They're involved in tremendous struggles and death-defying dramas. To reach enormousness, they depend on a complicated web of relationships, alliances and kinship networks.[2]

Wise old mother trees feed their saplings with liquid sugar and warn the neighbours when danger approaches. Reckless youngsters take foolhardy risks with leaf-shedding, light-chasing and excessive drinking, and usually pay with their lives. Crown Princes[3] wait for the old monarchs to fall, so they can take their place in the full glory of sunlight. It's all happening in the ultra-slow motion that is tree time, so that what we see is a freeze-frame of the action.

My guide here is a kind of tree whisperer. Peter Wohlleben, a German forester and author, has a rare understanding of the inner life of trees, and is able to describe it in accessible, evocative language. He stands very tall and straight, like the trees he most admires, and on this cold, clear morning, the blue of his eyes precisely matches the blue of the sky.

Wohlleben has devoted his life to the study and care of trees. He manages this forest as a nature reserve, and lives with his wife, Miriam, in a rustic cabin near the remote village of Hümmel.

Now, at the age of 53, he has become an unlikely publishing sensation. His book *The Hidden Life of Trees: What They Feel, How They Communicate*, written at his wife's insistence, sold more than 800,000 copies in Germany, and has now hit the best-seller lists in 11 other countries, including the United States and Canada.

Wohlleben sees a forest as a superorganism[4] of unique individuals. A single beech tree can live for years and produce 1.8 million beechnuts. A revolution has been taking place in the scientific understanding of trees, and Wohlleben is the first writer to convey its amazements to a general audience. The latest scientific studies, conducted at well-respected universities in Germany and around the world, confirm what he has long suspected from close observation in this forest: trees are far more alert, social, sophisticated – and even intelligent – than we thought.

With his big green boots crunching through fresh snow, and a dewdrop catching sunlight on the tip of his long nose, Wohlleben takes me to two massive beech trees growing next to each other. He points up at their skeletal[5] winter crowns, which appear careful not to encroach into each other's space. 'These two are old friends,' he says. 'They are very considerate in sharing the sunlight, and their root systems are closely connected. In cases like this, when one dies, the other usually dies soon afterward, because they are dependent on each other.'

Since Darwin,[6] we have generally thought of trees as striving, disconnected loners, competing for water, nutrients and sunlight, with the winners shading out the losers and sucking them dry. The timber industry in particular sees forests as wood-producing systems and battlegrounds for survival of the fittest.

There is now a substantial body[7] of scientific evidence that refutes that idea. It shows instead that trees of the same species are communal, and will often form alliances with trees of other species. Forest trees have evolved to live in cooperative, interdependent relationships, maintained by communication and a collective intelligence similar to an insect colony.

1. **unrestricted**
2. **close links**
3. **younger trees**
4. **system of living things**
5. **scrawny**
6. **Charles Darwin, naturalist**
7. **amount**

Close analysis of Richard Grant's language in the above extract provides readers with a greater understanding of the extract. The following discussion notes focus on **techniques used by the writer to convey his ideas**.

- In the opening paragraph, Grant invites readers to join him on a walk through the mountain forest. He establishes a dreamlike 'fairy tale' **sense of place** among the 'vibrantly alive' trees.

- Grant is immediately aware of this living natural 'tree time' world. His use of **personification** ('mother trees', 'youngsters') reflects the great respect he feels.

- Paragraph 3 describes the writer's adviser and guide, Peter Wohlleben. Does his **portrayal** seem realistic or idealistic? Is Grant ever likely to challenge any of Wohlleben's ideas?

- The focus then turns to summarising Wohlleben's own views of the forest as a **'superorganism'** and how trees are more 'intelligent' that previously thought.

- In the final paragraphs, **illustrations** are presented to support the idea that 'trees of the same species are communal'. Does Grant offer plausible and persuasive evidence or is it unconvincing?

SAMPLE PERSONAL RESPONSE QUESTION

QUESTION A

(ii)   In the extract, Peter Wohlleben observes that trees are far more social and intelligent than people think. Discuss the extent to which you agree or disagree with this observation.   **(15)**

   Allow about 15 minutes and aim for three focused, supported points in short paragraphs.

SAMPLE ANSWER

1. Peter Wohlleben is obviously an expert on trees, but I think he is almost emotionally involved with them. Although I know very little about trees or forests, I can't actually believe that they communicate with each other – and definitely not in the way that animals and humans do. I certainly don't agree that a word such as 'intelligent' can be used to describe trees. To me, this isn't realistic at all.

> First response – disagreeing that trees are intelligent or can communicate

2. But I would definitely agree that a forest of trees is very like a community in ways. For example, there are many different kinds of trees and at all ages. Some are strong but others are small and weak just as we read about in the extract. It's like a typical garden where some bushes and flowers might just be of better quality than others mostly by luck. In certain cases, for example, the amount of light or water will have a big effect on plant life.

> Agree that trees are like a social community in some ways

3. Like a lot of younger people, I learned about photosynthesis in biology and learned that trees are alive in one sense because they can grow and need water and air to survive. They are also affected by weather and tree diseases and all of them eventually decay and die. Overall, I think Peter Wohlleben is speaking in a symbolic way and definitely not claiming that forests are intelligent in human terms. And trees definitely don't communicate with people.

> Developed point that trees live and die – but not in the same way as humans

EXAMINER'S COMMENT

- Solid and focused personal response that tackles the question and challenges Wohlleben's views.

- Some good development of key points to support arguments – particularly in paragraphs two and three.

- Expression is generally clear, but slightly repetitive (e.g. 'definitely' is over-used).

- The second last sentence rounds off the response effectively. **(12/15)**

NOTE

The term 'an insight' in Comprehending A questions means a new realisation or idea you discover when reading the text. Insights usually refer to new knowledge that you gain.

CLASS/HOMEWORK ACTIVITY

QUESTION A

(i) Based on your reading of the above extract, explain three insights you gain from Richard Grant and Peter Wohlleben into trees and forests. Support your answer with reference to the text. **(15)**

🕐 **Allow about 15 minutes and aim to write three focused, supported points in short paragraphs.**

Learning aim: To analyse and discuss key features of gothic writing

GOTHIC FICTION

- Gothic literature is a genre of fiction from the end of the 18th century. The term 'Gothic' originates from the name of an ancient Germanic tribe (the Goths) who had a reputation for being barbaric.

- There are numerous Gothic elements in the novel *Frankenstein*, including desolate settings, dark secrets, troubled characters and the imminent threat of the monster.

- Gothic stories create a melodramatic atmosphere of tension using mystery, fear and dread rather than relying on violence and bloodshed to scare the reader.

GOTHIC WRITING STYLISTIC FEATURES

○ **Gloomy setting** ○ **Eerie atmosphere** ○ **Horrific events** ○ **Dark secrets** ○ **Unstable central character** ○ **Supernatural elements – ghosts or monsters** ○ **Fascination with death** ○ **Grotesque descriptive details** ○ **Disturbing sense of terror and suspense**

FRANKENSTEIN

This text is taken from Mary Shelley's novel, *Frankenstein*, written in 1818. The young scientist, Victor Frankenstein, describes the night he completes his experiment. After months of work, using body parts from deceased criminals, he finally succeeds in creating a living creature.

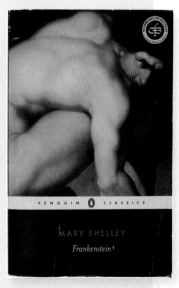

Read the following extract carefully, paying particular attention to the writer's style.

It was on a dreary night of November that I beheld the accomplishment of my toils.[1] With an anxiety that almost amounted to agony, collected the instruments of life around me, that I might infuse[2] a spark of being into the lifeless thing that lay at my feet. It was already one in the morning; the rain pattered dismally against the panes, and my candle was nearly burnt out, when, by the glimmer of the half-extinguished light, I saw the dull yellow eye of the creature open; it breathed hard, and a convulsive[3] motion agitated its limbs.

How can I describe my emotions at this catastrophe, or how delineate[4] the wretch whom with such infinite pains and care I had endeavoured to form? His limbs were in proportion, and I had selected his features as beautiful. Beautiful! – Great God! His yellow skin scarcely covered the work of muscles and arteries beneath; his hair was of a lustrous black, and flowing; his teeth of pearly whiteness; but these luxuriances only formed a more horrid contrast with his watery eyes, that seemed almost of the same colour as the dun white sockets in which they were set, his shrivelled complexion and straight black lips.

The different accidents of life are not so changeable as the feelings of human nature. I had worked hard for nearly two years, for the sole purpose of infusing life into an inanimate body. For this I had deprived myself of rest and health. I had desired it with an ardour[5] that far exceeded moderation; but now that I had finished, the beauty of the dream vanished, and breathless horror and disgust filled my heart. Unable to endure the aspect of the being I had created, I rushed out of the room and continued a long time traversing my bedchamber, unable to compose my mind to sleep. At length lassitude[6] succeeded to the tumult I had before endured, and I threw myself on the bed in my clothes, endeavouring to seek a few moments of forgetfulness.

But I was in vain; I slept, indeed, but I was disturbed by the wildest dreams. I thought I saw Elizabeth, in the bloom of health, walking in the streets of Ingolstadt.[7] Delighted and surprised, I embraced her, but as I imprinted the first kiss on her lips, they became livid[8] with the hue of death; her features appeared to change, and I thought that I held the corpse of my dead mother in my arms; a shroud enveloped her form, and I saw the grave-worms crawling in the folds of the flannel.

I started from my sleep with horror; a cold dew covered my forehead, my teeth chattered, and every limb became convulsed; when, by the dim and yellow light of the moon, as it forced its way through the window shutters, I beheld the wretch – the miserable monster whom I had created. He held up the curtain of the bed; and his eyes, if eyes they may be called, were fixed on me. His jaws opened, and he muttered some inarticulate sounds, while a grin wrinkled his cheeks. He might have spoken, but I did not hear; one hand was stretched out, seemingly to detain me, but I escaped and rushed downstairs.

1. **efforts**
2. **introduce**
3. **shuddering**
4. **describe**
5. **passion**
6. **tiredness**
7. **German city**
8. **discoloured**

Close analysis of the use of language in a text is essential for answering questions successfully. The following discussion notes focus on key words and phrases that illustrate **Mary Shelley's Gothic writing skill**.

- The month of November is often associated with death. Shelley's 'dreary night' **setting** and bleak weather ('rain pattered dismally') add to the miserable tone.

- Victor Frankenstein is intensely horrified by the **morbid imagery** used to describe 'the wretch' with its 'dull yellow eye' and 'shrivelled complexion'.

- The author makes effective **use of irony** to highlight Victor's shocked reaction to the creature's ugliness. He retreats to his bedchamber and tries to sleep but has a terrible dream in which his bride-to-be appears as his mother's corpse.

- Shelley's vivid description heightens the **disturbing atmosphere** in the scene. References to 'grave-worms' and 'my teeth chattered' are melodramatic, emphasising the sense of terror.

- There is a heightened sense of **suspense** throughout the extract, leading to Frankenstein's desperate escape at the end.

SAMPLE QUESTION ON GOTHIC STYLE

QUESTION A

(iii) Identify four elements of the writer's style in the above extract and discuss how effectively these stylistic elements are used to craft a powerful piece of Gothic horror literature. Support your answer with reference to the text.

(20)

SAMPLE ANSWER

1. In the extract it is clear that Mary Shelley uses a gothic horror style to show the birth of the 'being' described as 'the miserable monster'. Also as 'the wretch'. Even though Victor Frankenstein's creature is alive, it's described as if it was a corpse with 'black lips' and 'watery eyes'. This is typical of horror literature and makes a powerful impact by terrifying readers. Gothic stories are often about dead bodies coming to life, so this is a good example of this kind of writing.

> First style element – vivid description
>
> Effect – terrifies reader

2. Another horror or gothic feature is the terrified main character of mad scientist who is out of control. The narrator was planning on creating a 'beautiful' creature. But the exact opposite happened. He knows he has done wrong and is almost driven mad after seeing the ugly monster, 'I was disturbed by the wildest dreams'.

> Second element – characterisation of scientist
>
> Effect – irony of unintended outcome

3. A third horror element is the night time atmosphere for this gothic story. The monster is described as coming alive at 'one in the morning' in the darkness – 'the glimmer of the half-extinguished light'. The whole mood is mysterious and spooky ('the dim and yellow light of the moon'), so that readers are probably scared of what will happen next. The suspense increases as the scientist now understands his 'catastrophe'. He has abused his power by creating this unnatural creature who turns against him – 'His jaws opened'.

> Third element – night-time atmosphere
>
> Effect – creates scary mood

4. In conclusion, gothic settings are traditionally creepy and this plays a part in creating suspense. The tense mood in the extract gets more and more scary and menacing as it is described towards the end. The narrator is haunted by the monster's weird 'grin' and is desperate to escape – 'rushed downstairs'.

> Fourth element – creepy setting
>
> Effect – creates mood of suspense

EXAMINER'S COMMENT

- Focused response that includes some interesting insights into Shelley's language use.
- Well-developed discussion of the effective description of the monster and the dark atmosphere throughout the extract.
- Relevant quotations and references support discussion and illustrate the powerful writing.
- Although some points overlap slightly and the expression is repetitive at times ('creating', 'described'), there is a good overall understanding of the writer's Gothic style. **(17/20)**

CLASS/HOMEWORK ACTIVITY

QUESTION A

(i) Based on your reading of the extract above, explain three insights you gain into the character of Victor Frankenstein. Support your response with reference to the text. **(15)**

🕐 **Allow about 15 minutes and aim for three focused, supported points in short paragraphs.**

PROMPT

- Victor Frankenstein – idealistic scientist or misguided genius?
- Was his experiment sensible or reckless and irresponsible?
- Is he an unstable and dangerous character?
- Does his reaction to the creature reveal weakness?
- Was Victor a villain or victim? Or both?

5 Analysing Setting

Learning aim: To analyse and discuss key aspects of setting

WRITING ABOUT SETTING

● Setting refers to the **time, place and circumstances** when events occur. The setting can play a significant part in a text, establishing atmosphere and reflecting themes and character.

● Writers make **use of all five senses** (sight, sound, smell, taste and touch) to describe settings and involve readers in a story.

● Characters can sometimes be **in conflict with the setting**, e.g. battling hostile locations or harsh weather conditions.

● **Social setting** is just as important as the **physical location**. It refers to the **'world' of the text**. This includes social class, culture, attitudes and beliefs of characters, etc. In *The Great Gatsby*, for example, we learn about the lives of people in America during the 1920s.

● The **atmosphere or mood** created by the setting can be revealing. Is it positive, cheerful, gloomy, mysterious, threatening, etc.?

SETTING – SOME STYLISTIC FEATURES

○ **Detailed description**   ○ **Vivid language**   ○ **Personification (the setting is treated like a character)**   ○ **Evocative atmosphere**   ○ **Suggestion**   ○ **Use of pathetic fallacy (where the environment and weather reflect the mood)**

THE GREAT GATSBY

This text is from F. Scott Fitzgerald's novel, *The Great Gatsby*. The story begins in 1922 when Nick Carraway rents a small house on Long Island, New York. The mansion next door belongs to the millionaire, Jay Gatsby. In this extract, Carraway describes weekend parties at the mansion of his mysterious neighbour.

Read the extract carefully, paying particular attention to how the writer establishes setting and atmosphere.

There was music from my neighbour's house through the summer nights. In his blue gardens men and girls came and went like moths among the whisperings and the champagne and the stars. At high tide in the afternoon I watched his guests diving from the tower of his raft, or taking the sun on the hot sand of his beach while his two motor-boats slit the waters of the Sound,[1] drawing aquaplanes over cataracts[2] of foam. On weekends his Rolls-Royce became an omnibus, bearing parties to and from the city between nine in the morning and long past midnight, while his station wagon scampered like a brisk yellow bug to meet all trains.

And on Mondays eight servants, including an extra gardener, toiled all day with mops and scrubbing-brushes and hammers and garden-shears, repairing the ravages[3] of the night before.

Every Friday five crates of oranges and lemons arrived from a fruiterer in New York – every Monday these same oranges and lemons left his back door in a pyramid of pulpless halves. There was a machine in the kitchen which could extract the juice of two hundred oranges in half an hour if a little button was pressed two hundred times by a butler's thumb.

At least once a fortnight a corps[4] of caterers came down with several hundred feet of canvas and enough coloured lights to make a Christmas tree of Gatsby's enormous garden. On buffet tables, garnished with glistening hors-d'oeuvre, spiced baked hams crowded against salads of harlequin[5] designs and pastry pigs and turkeys bewitched to a dark gold. In the main hall a bar with a real brass rail was set up, and stocked with gins and liquors and with cordials so long forgotten that most of his female guests were too young to know one from another.

By seven o'clock the orchestra has arrived, no thin five-piece affair, but a whole pitful of oboes and trombones and saxophones and viols and cornets and piccolos, and low and high drums. The last swimmers have come in from the beach now and are dressing upstairs; the cars from New York are parked five deep in the drive,

and already the halls and salons and verandas are gaudy with primary colours, and hair shorn in strange new ways, and shawls beyond the dreams of Castile.[6] The bar is in full swing, and floating rounds of cocktails permeate the garden outside, until the air is alive with chatter and laughter, and casual innuendo[7] and introductions forgotten on the spot, and enthusiastic meetings between women who never knew each other's names.

The lights grow brighter as the earth lurches away from the sun, and now the orchestra is playing yellow cocktail music, and the opera of voices pitches a key higher. Laughter is easier minute by minute, spilled with prodigality,[8] tipped out at a cheerful word. The groups change more swiftly, swell with new arrivals, dissolve and form in the same breath; already there are wanderers, confident girls who weave here and there among the stouter and more stable, become for a sharp, joyous moment the centre of a group, and then, excited with triumph, glide on through the sea-change of faces and voices and colour under the constantly changing light.

Suddenly one of the gypsies, in trembling opal,[9] seizes a cocktail out of the air, dumps it down for courage and, moving her hands like Frisco,[10] dances out alone on the canvas platform. A momentary hush; the orchestra leader varies his rhythm obligingly for her, and there is a burst of chatter as the erroneous news goes around that she is Gilda Gray's understudy from the Follies.[11] The party has begun.

1. **inlet or bay**
2. **surges**
3. **damage**
4. **group**
5. **flamboyant**
6. **Spanish castle**
7. **gossip**
8. **wastefulness**
9. **sequinned dress**
10. **American dancer**
11. **New York musical**

Close analysis of language use in the text is essential for answering questions successfully.

- The opening paragraph introduces readers to Gatsby's 'blue gardens', a **dreamlike world of luxury and extravagance**. Fitzgerald's language conveys the beautiful but short-term nature of how some wealthy Americans partied during the 1920s.

- **The party guests are compared to 'moths'** – insects that drift mindlessly towards the nearest bright light.

- The physical setting provides a backdrop for Gatsby's fashionable 'world'. Detailed descriptions of the **setting establishes a privileged atmosphere** and showy displays of wealth, such as 'his beach' and 'his Rolls-Royce'.

- **Symbols** expose Gatsby's over-indulgent and wasteful lifestyle. His home is 'gaudy with primary colours'. Almost everything about the mansion is **vulgar and tasteless**, reflecting the corruption beneath all the glitz and glamour. The party itself symbolises the shallow values of high society at the time.

- While the extract captures the freedom and exuberance of the 'Roaring Twenties', Fitzgerald highlights an advantaged social class whose lives are **hedonistic and self-gratifying**.

- There is lots of energetic dancing and insincere 'chatter' – and the 'bar is in full swing' (even though drinking was illegal due to prohibition laws). The **shameless disregard for rules** is another telling aspect of this culture.

- Our appreciation of the novel is informed by Fitzgerald's **use of setting**. He leaves readers in no doubt that Gatsby's party-goers are desperate to be 'the centre of a group' for one 'joyous moment'. Their empty lives are tinged with sadness.

NOTE

In Comprehending questions, an **observation** usually refers to something that is noted as a result of experience.

Writers or characters often notice things that attract their attention. For example, a written guide to Dublin Zoo will include interesting observations about animal behaviour.

CLASS/HOMEWORK ACTIVITY

QUESTION A

(i) Based on your reading of the above extract, identify and explain three observations that F. Scott Fitzgerald makes that are critical of American society at the time in which the novel is set. Support your answer with reference to the text. **(15)**

Allow about 15 minutes and aim for three focused, supported points in short paragraphs. The notes above may be helpful in responding to the question.

WRITING ABOUT STYLE

- Style is **the way a writer uses words** to suit a specific purpose, context or audience.

- Language, diction (word choice), imagery, syntax (the order of words) and sentence fluency all shape the style of a piece of writing, **contributing to mood** and meaning.

- The **writer's unique voice** is another essential element of style. The tone can be personal or formal, authoritative or reflective, objective or passionate, serious or humorous, etc.

- When reading a text, you will quickly become aware of how that particular writer uses language. A **pattern may emerge** where a certain technique is repeated.

- In the extract that follows from *Life of Pi*, the author varies the length of sentences to help create **different moods**. For example, short disjointed sentences reflect the panic-stricken atmosphere on the sinking ship.

LIFE OF PI

The following text is from *Life of Pi*, a fantasy novel by Yann Martel. In this extract, Pi is aboard a ship which is carrying animals belonging to his father, who owns a zoo.

Read the following extract carefully, paying particular attention to the writer's language use.

Inside the ship, there were noises. Deep structural[1] groans. I stumbled and fell. No harm done. I got up. With the help of the handrails I went down the stairwell four steps at a time. I had gone down just one level when I saw water. Lots of water. It was blocking my way. It was surging from below like a riotous crowd, raging, frothing and boiling. Stairs vanished into watery darkness. I couldn't believe my eyes. What was this water doing here? Where had it come from? I stood nailed to the spot, frightened and incredulous and ignorant of what I should do next. Down there was where my family was.

I ran up the stairs. I got to the main deck. The weather wasn't entertaining any more. I was very afraid. Now it was plain and obvious: the ship was listing[2] badly. And it wasn't level the other way either. There was a noticeable incline going from bow[3] to stern.[4] I looked overboard. The water didn't look to be eighty feet away. The ship was sinking. My mind could hardly conceive it. It was as unbelievable as the moon catching fire.

Where were the officers and the crew? What were they doing? Towards the bow I saw some men running in the gloom. I thought I saw some animals too, but I dismissed the sight as illusion crafted by rain and shadow. We had the hatch covers over their bay pulled open when the weather was good, but at all times the animals were kept confined to their cages. These were dangerous wild animals we were transporting, not farm livestock. Above me, on the bridge,[5] I thought I heard some men shouting.

The ship shook and there was that sound, the monstrous metallic burp. What was it? Was it the collective scream of humans and animals protesting their oncoming death? Was it the ship itself giving up the ghost? I fell over. I got to my feet. I looked overboard again. The sea was rising. The waves were getting closer. We were sinking fast.

I clearly heard monkeys shrieking. Something was shaking the deck, a gaur – an Indian wild ox – exploded out of the rain and thundered by me, terrified, out of control, berserk. I looked at it, dumbstruck and amazed. Who in God's name had let it out?

I ran for the stairs to the bridge. Up there was where the officers were, the only people on the ship who spoke English, the masters of our destiny here, the ones who would right this wrong. They would explain everything. They would take care of my family and me. I climbed to the middle bridge. There was no one on the starboard[6] side. I ran to the port[7] side. I saw three men, crew members. I fell. I got up. They were looking overboard. I shouted. They turned. They looked at me and at each other. They spoke a few words. They came towards me quickly. I felt gratitude and relief welling up in me. I said, 'Thank God I've found you. What is happening? I am very scared. There is water at the bottom of the ship. I am worried about my family. I can't get to the level where our cabins are. Is this normal? Do you think-'

One of the men interrupted me by thrusting a life jacket into my arms and shouting something in Chinese. I noticed an orange whistle dangling from the life jacket. The men were nodding vigorously at me. When they took hold of me and lifted me in their strong arms, I thought nothing of it. I thought they were helping me. I was so full of trust in them that I felt grateful as they carried me in the air. Only when they threw me overboard did I begin to have doubts.

1. **physical**
2. **leaning to the left**
3. **front**
4. **rear**
5. **control room**
6. **right-hand side**
7. **left-hand side**

NOTE

In Comprehending questions, an **element** of style usually refers to a characteristic or distinctive feature of how the writer uses language. For example, some writers include a lot of dialogue, others use vivid symbols or detailed description, etc.

SAMPLE COMPREHENDING A STYLE QUESTION

QUESTION A

(iii) Identify four elements of Yann Martel's writing style evident in the extract above and discuss how effectively these elements are employed to craft a tense and dramatic account of Pi's experience aboard the sinking ship. Support your answer with reference to the text. **(20)**

SAMPLE ANSWER

1. Yann Martel's style is very detailed. The first feature I found he uses lots of vivid images to show the total chaos on the sinking ship. He describes the sea water as 'frothing and boiling'. This suggests confusion and anxiety on board. It's interesting that Pi noticed the 'orange whistle dangling from the life jacket'. This small detail is a good reminder of the serious danger facing him after leaving the ship. And going into the sea.

> First stylistic element – detailed writing
>
> Effect – dramatic impact

2. Martel uses short snappy sentences and questions to highlight Pi's panic, 'I stumbled and fell', 'I fell', 'I got up'. He repeats 'I got up' which suggests Pi's confusion and struggle as he runs around searching desperately for his family. This really gives a sense of the dramatic atmosphere. All the questions going through his mind increase the tension. Pi really doesn't know what to do and is in a state of utter panic, 'What was this water doing here?', 'Who in God's name had let it out?', 'What is happening? 'The questions made me feel really sorry for him.

> Second feature – short sentences/questions
>
> Effect – intensifies concern for the character

3. The writer also shows the ship as a living creature just like the terrified animals. He describes the noises as 'groans' coming from the bottom of the ship. It 'shook' and gave a 'monstrous metallic burp'. He wonders if the ship is dying, 'giving up the ghost'. This adds to the terror and drama, almost like a nightmare. I got the impression of Pi's helplessness and that he feels under very great pressure and almost haunted since everything is beyond his control.

> Third element – personification of ship
>
> Effect – creates nightmare scene

4. The fourth writing element I found crafting a tense and dramatic account of Pi's experience aboard the sinking ship was tense exaggeration and this can go over the top with dramatic statements. For an example, he describes the water as being 'like a riotous crowd'. And then says a 'wild ox exploded out of the rain'. This exaggeration could show how very terrified and tense he feels.

> Fourth feature – exaggeration
>
> Effect – increases tension

EXAMINER'S COMMENT

- Focuses well on style and engages closely with the tension and drama in the extract.

- Perceptive points on discussion on effect of detail, short sentences and personification.

- Discussion supported throughout with suitable reference.

- Quotations are very well integrated into the commentary.

- Expression slightly awkward at times, e.g. in the less effective final paragraph. **(18/20)**

CLASS/HOMEWORK ACTIVITY

QUESTION A

(i) Based on your reading of the extract, explain three insights you gain into Pi's character and personality. Support your answer with reference to the text. **(15)**

 Allow about 15 minutes and aim for three focused, supported points.

PROMPT

!

- What is your first impression of Pi?

- How does he respond in a crisis?

- Is he keen to survive at all costs?

- Does he show concern for other people?

- In dealing with strangers, is he careful or naïve?

- Is he observant? Engaging? Brave? Smart?

Learning aim: To analyse and discuss key features of crime writing

CRIME FICTION

● Crime fiction has been hugely popular since the early 1800s. As the term clearly implies, this genre is largely classified by stories that are centred around the **solving of a serious crime**, such as murder.

● Among the **many types of crime and detective fiction** are 'Whodunits', police and/or private investigations, courtroom dramas and serial killer cases. Forensic thrillers involve a pathologist or scientist examining evidence left at the crime scene.

● Crime, mysteries and thrillers are usually **suspenseful and full of intrigue**. In many of these novels, of course, things aren't always what they seem.

● Detective genre elements often include a **realistic storyline** involving a significant crime, a **central character** determined to solve the case, a **number of suspects** and, ultimately, the **criminal** must be revealed.

A QUESTION OF IDENTITY

The passage below is taken from Susan Hill's novel, _A Question of Identity_. The scene is a Yorkshire courtroom where Alan Keyes has pleaded not guilty to the murder of three elderly women. Two crime reporters, Charlie Vogt and Rod Hawkins, wait to hear the verdict, fully expecting the accused man to be convicted.

Read the following extract carefully, paying particular attention to the writer's language use.

The court was full to overflowing, the public benches packed. Charlie and Rod stood pressed against the doors poised like greyhounds in the slips.[1]

You never got over it, Charlie thought, your blood pressure went up with the tension and excitement. Better than any film, better than any book. There was just nothing to beat it, watching the drama of the court, eyes on the face of the accused when the word rang out. Guilty. The look of the relatives, as they flushed with joy, relief, exhaustion. And then the tears. These were the final moments when he knew why he was in his job. Every time.

Alan Keyes stood, face pale, eyes down, his police minder impassive.

Charlie's throat constricted[2] suddenly as he looked at him, looked at his hands on the rail. Normal hands. Nothing ugly, nothing out of the ordinary. Not a strangler's hands, whatever they were supposed to look like. But the hands, resting on the rail, hands like his own, one beside the other resting on the rail, resting on the … those hands had … Charlie did not think of himself as hard-boiled[3] but you did get accustomed. But nothing prepared you for the first time you saw the man in front of you, ordinary, innocent until proved guilty, however clear his guilt was, nothing prepared you for the sight of a man like Keyes, there in the flesh, a man who had strangled three elderly women. Nothing. He couldn't actually look at Keyes at all now.

The lawyers sat together, shuffling papers, fiddling with box lids, not looking at one another, not murmuring. Just waiting.

And then the door opened and they were filing back, concentrating on taking their seats, faces showing the strain, or else blank and showing nothing at all. Seven women, five men. Charlie was struck by the expression on the face of the first woman, young with dark hair pulled tightly back, bright red scarf round her neck. She looked desperate – desperate to get out? Desperate because she was afraid? Desperate not to catch the eye of the man in the dock,[4] the ordinary-looking man with the unremarkable hands who had strangled three old women?

Charlie watched as she sat down and stared straight ahead of her, glazed, tired. What had she done to deserve the past nine days, hearing appalling things, looking at terrible images? Been a citizen. Nothing else. He had often wondered how people like her coped when it had all been forgotten, but the images and the accounts wouldn't leave their heads. Once you knew something you couldn't un-know it. His Dad had tried to un-know what he'd learned about Hindley and Brady[5] for years afterwards.

'All rise.'

The court murmured; the murmur faded. Everything went still. Every eye focused on the jury benches.

In the centre of the public benches a knot of elderly women sat together. Two had their hands on one another's arms. Even across the room, Charlie Vogt could see a pulse jumping in the neck of one, the pallor[6] of her neighbour. Behind them, two middle-aged couples, one with a young woman. He knew relatives when he saw them, very quiet, very still, desperate for this to be over, to see justice being done. Hang in there, he willed them, a few minutes and then you walk away, to try and put your lives back together.

Schoolteacher, he thought, as the foreman of the jury stood. Bit young, no more than early thirties. Several of them looked even younger. When he'd done jury service himself, several years ago now, there had only been two women and the men had all been late-middle-aged.

'Have you reached a verdict on all three counts?'

'Yes.'

'On the first count, do you find the accused guilty or not guilty?' The first murder of Carrie Gage.

Charlie realised that he was clenching his hand, digging his nails into the palm.

'Not guilty.'

The intake of breath was like a sigh round the room.

'Is this a unanimous[7] verdict?'

'Yes.'

'On the second count of murder, do you find the accused guilty or not guilty?' Sarah Pearce.

'Not guilty.'

The murmur was faint, like a tide coming in. Charlie glanced at the faces of the legal teams. Impassive except for the junior barrister of the defence who had put her hands briefly to her mouth.

'Is this verdict unanimous?'

'Yes.'

'On the third count, do you find the accused guilty or not guilty?'

His honour Judge Palmer was sitting very straight, hands out of sight, expression unreadable.

'Not guilty.'

'Is – '

The gavel came down hard on the bench and the judge's voice roared out:

'Order …'

1. **ready to race**
2. **tightened**
3. **cold-hearted**
4. **on trial**
5. **two notorious murderers**
6. **pale appearance**
7. **agreed by the jury**

CRIME WRITING STYLISTIC FEATURES

- ○ **Compelling plot**
- ○ **Memorable characters**
- ○ **Suspense and conflict**
- ○ **Vivid description**
- ○ **Tense atmosphere**
- ○ **Foreshadowing**
- ○ **Haunting settings**

Close analysis of language use in the text is essential for answering questions successfully. The following discussion notes focus on key words and phrases that illustrate the writer's skill.

- The extract opens with a description of the 'overflowing' courtroom just before the verdict is to be announced. Relatives of the victims are anxious. **Details create a sense of anticipation**, which is compared to the start of a greyhound race.

- **Readers share the tension** through the experience of the reporter, Charlie Vogt, whose thoughts focus on the accused man – and how his hands ('hands like his own') strangled three women. But is Alan Keyes actually guilty or not?

- The **court trial is an important element of the crime writing genre** as readers are interested in justice – 'Every eye focused on the jury benches'.

- **Susan Hill creates further uneasiness** through delaying the jury's verdict by concentrating again Charlie's viewpoint. We see the jury and various other people in court through his eyes.

- The names of two of the victims are revealed, Sarah Pearce and Carrie Gage. Does this make us sympathise with them more? Do we become **more involved in the drama**?

- When the 'not guilty' verdicts are given one by one, there is a feeling of shock and numbness. But is there also a suggestion of disquiet and anger. **Unexpected twists and turns** are another feature of crime writing.

- The **scene ends on an uncomfortable** note ('the judge's voice roared out'), leaving readers to wonder what might happen in the future – particularly if a murderer is still free to kill again.

CLASS/HOMEWORK ACTIVITY

QUESTION A

(iii) Based on your reading of the extract from *A Question of Identity*, identify four elements of the writer's style and discuss how effectively these stylistic elements are used to craft a tense and atmospheric piece of crime fiction. Support your answer with reference to the text.

(20)

🕐 **Allow about 20 minutes and aim to write four focused, supported points.**

- What makes the courtroom setting dramatic?
- How do Charlie's thoughts add to the sense of drama?
- Do the various characters contribute to the suspense?
- What is the impact of the repeated references to Alan Keyes' hands?
- How does the dialogue between the judge and jury foreman increase tension?

Learning aim: To analyse key features of successful travel writing

- Travel writing is a popular form of **non-fiction** which introduces readers to new places, people and culture.

- Modern-day travel pieces usually appear in blogs, newspaper and magazine articles, with a **focus on the writer's experience,** advice and must-sees.

- Much more **detailed accounts** of journeys or places can also be written in book form.

SOME TRAVEL WRITING FEATURES:

- Often written in first-person narrative, using 'I'

- Contains sensory details (sights, sounds, tastes, smells, etc.)

- Provides useful facts, insights and tourist tips

- Entertains readers with a creative writing style

- Engaging tone – conversational, humorous, enthusiastic, etc.

ANALYSING TRAVEL ARTICLES

Kate McCulley is a well-known solo travel blogger. Her website, *Adventurous Kate*, **resembles a personal journal. She uses lots of photos (which she takes herself) throughout her posts.**

Read this introduction to Kate's blog about Naples, and briefly answer the five short questions that follow.

Naples is one of my favourite places in Italy – and the world. This wild and fascinating city is chaotic, affordable and friendly. I can't get enough of it, and I'm always thinking about my next visit.

There are so many cool things to do in Naples Italy, no matter what kind of traveller you are. (Honestly, if you did nothing but eat pizza the entire time, I would get it! It's that good!)

Of course, you have cathedrals and museums and piazzas — but you also have fantastic pastries, interesting museums, and a looming volcano in the background!

Beyond the city itself, Naples is perfectly positioned for some of the best day trips in Italy, from Pompeii to Capri to the Amalfi Coast.

But for me, what makes Naples special is the energy. It's wonderfully unpretentious, full of locals who are gregarious and welcoming. And they don't rebuild their city to cater to tourists – they know what a special place they have, and that it should be appreciated for what it is.

Naples is incredible, and I can't wait to show you the best of the city Italians call Napoli.

CLASS/HOMEWORK ACTIVITY

(Suitable for group discussion or five short written exercises)

1. **What is the purpose** of Kate McCulley's article? (Informing, persuading, entertaining, etc.)
2. **Who is the target audience?** (Age group, gender, background, interests, etc.)
3. **What kind of language is used?** (Informative, formal, humorous, persuasive, etc.)
4. **What is the tone of the piece?** (Serious, chatty, personal, enthusiastic, etc.)
5. **Would this introduction make you want to read on?** Briefly explain your response.

NEITHER HERE NOR THERE

This piece of travel writing about a visit to Naples is taken from *Neither Here Nor There* by Bill Bryson.

Read the following extract carefully, paying particular attention to the writer's style.

I awoke to a gloomy day. The hillsides behind the town were obscured by a wispy haze and Naples across the bay appeared to have been taken away in the night. There was nothing but a plane of Dead Sea and beyond it the sort of tumbling fog that creatures from beyond the grave stumble out of in B-movies.[1] I had intended to walk to the hilltop ruins of Tiberius's[2] villa, where the old rascal used to have guests who displeased him hurled over the ramparts[3] onto the rocks hundreds of feet below, but when I emerged from the hotel a cold, slicing rain was falling, and I spent the morning wandering from café to café, drinking cappuccinos and scanning the sky. Late in the morning, out of time to see the villa unless I stayed another day, which I could scarce afford to do, I checked reluctantly out of the Hotel Capri and walked down the steep and slippery steps to the quay where I purchased a ticket on a slow ferry to Naples.

Naples looked even worse after Sorrento and Capri than it had before. I walked for half a mile along the waterfront, but there was no sign of happy fishermen mending their nets and singing 'Santa Lucia',[4] as I had fervently hoped there might be. Instead there were just menacing-looking derelicts[5] and mountains – and I mean mountains – of rubbish on every corner and yet more people selling lottery tickets and trinkets from cardboard boxes.

I had no map and only the vaguest sense of the geography of the city, but I turned inland hoping that I would blunder onto some shady square lined with small but decent hotels.

Surely even Naples must have its finer corners. Instead I found precisely the sort of streets that you automatically associate with Naples – mean, cavernous, semi-paved alleyways, with plaster peeling off walls and washing hung like banners between balconies that never saw sunlight. The streets were full of overplump women and unattended children, often naked from the waist down, in filthy T-shirts.

I felt as if I had wandered onto another continent. In the centre of Naples some 70,000 families live even now in cramped *bassi* – tenements without baths or running water, sometimes without even a window, with up to fifteen members of an extended family living together in a single room. The worst of these districts, the *Vicaria*, where I was now, is said to have the highest population density in Europe, possibly in the world, now that the Forbidden City in Hong Kong is being demolished. And it has crime to match – especially the pettier crimes like car theft (29,000 in one year) and muggings.

Yet I felt safe enough. No one paid any attention to me, except occasionally to give me a stray smile. I was clearly a tourist with my rucksack, and I confess I clutched the straps tightly, but there was no sign of the *scippatori*,[6] the famous bag snatchers on Vespas[7] who doubtless sensed that all they would get was some dirty underpants, half a bar of chocolate and a tattered copy of H. V. Morton's *A Traveller in Southern Italy*.

1. **low-budget films, often horror**
2. **a Roman emperor**
3. **high walls**
4. **traditional song from Naples**
5. **run-down buildings**
6. **thieves**
7. **mopeds**

SAMPLE QUESTION

(i) Based on your reading of the above extract, identify and explain three insights that you gain into the writer's character and personality. Support your answer with reference to the text.

(15)

🕐 **Allow about 15 minutes and aim for three focused, supported points.**

SAMPLE ANSWER

1. I thought Bill Bryson had a very one-sided attitude to Italy. He seems to me to be determined to have a bad time. If it's not the weather, it's the steep steps he has to walk down. Bryson is really narrow-minded about a completely different culture which doesn't match where he comes from. He also complains constantly, e.g. about the 'slow ferry'. No wonder he is travelling on his own.

> First characteristic – Bryson's narrow-minded attitude
>
> Insight – Explains why he has no friends

2. When he gets to Naples, he notices everything that's wrong about the place and just expects to see happy smiling fishermen. He gets really annoyed by the 'mountains' of rubbish. This is obvious exaggeration and there was probably a strike at the time which is common in most big cities. I thought he was totally irrational in making little or no effort to understand another completely different culture. His mean description of the 'overplump women and unattended children' and their 'filthy T-shirts' came close to crossing a line, in my opinion.

> Second characteristic – He seems constantly annoyed.
>
> Insight – Suggests that he's not a positive person

3. To be fair, he showed a better understanding of a deprived inner urban area towards the end. He seemed more aware of the reality of life under pressure, e.g. the 'extended family living together in a single room'. But he really contradicts himself in quoting stats about muggings while then saying he himself was 'safe enough'. Overall, I saw a few different sides to Bill's character but although he has a sense of humour, I wouldn't want to be travelling with him.

> Third characteristic – Some awareness of the real Naples
>
> Insight – Shows Bryson's more sympathetic character

EXAMINER'S COMMENT

- Focuses well on several of the writer's character traits, using supportive reference and quotation.

- Points are generally coherent and clearly argued – apart from an unconvincing comment regarding contradiction in the final paragraph.

- Expression is lively and reasonably controlled – although there is some repetition (e.g. 'really', 'a completely different culture').

- Solid response, overall, includes some good engagement with the text. **(13/15)**

WORD POWER

Close analysis of language use in the text is essential for answering questions successfully. The following discussion notes focus on key words and phrases that illustrate the writer's skill:

- Bill Bryson's opening description of the **unappealing setting** ('gloomy day', 'dead sea') suggests his downbeat mood.

- Use of the first-person narrative forms an immediate connection with readers and his **light-hearted anecdote** (story) about 'the old rascal' Tiberius establishes a chatty tone.

- The writer's **harshly critical view** of Naples is in stark contrast to the usual 'picture postcard' tourist image – 'even worse after Sorrento', 'no sign of happy fishermen'.

- **Graphic description** of discarded street rubbish partly explains why he is so negative.

- **Further details** of his walk through 'the mean, cavernous, semi-paved alleyways' emphasise his disappointment.

- Cinematic images of city life create a sense of the **hectic, bustling atmosphere**.

- In the third paragraph, Bryson focuses on the deprived **social conditions** in some impoverished areas – 'tenements without baths or running water'. Has his tone changed?

- The extract ends on a personal note which **seems to reflect his honesty and impartiality** – 'I felt safe enough'. Yet questions remain about whether the writer's view of Naples is balanced and fair-minded.

- In the end, this extract may well engage readers, but is **unlikely to persuade** them to visit the city.

QUESTION A

(iii) What features of Bill Bryson's style make this an informative and engaging piece of travel writing? Support your answer with reference to the text. **(20)**

 Allow about 20 minutes to write four focused, supported points in short paragraphs. The notes above may be helpful in responding to the question.

TRAVEL QUOTES

I haven't been everywhere, but it's on my list.
Susan Sontag

To shut your eyes is to travel.
Emily Dickinson

Life is either a daring adventure or nothing at all.
Helen Keller

If you think adventure is dangerous, try routine – it's lethal.
Paulo Coelho

Travel, of course, narrows the mind.
Malcolm Muggeridge

Not all those who wander are lost.
J. R. R. Tolkien

I am not a great cook, I am not a great artist, but I love art and I love food; so I am the perfect traveller.
Michael Palin

LESSON 9 Responding to Informative Texts

Learning aim: To analyse and discuss key features of informative writing

- Informative language aims to **communicate information** clearly and concisely. The purpose is to explain a topic and convey ideas to readers without bias (opinion).

- The writer is simply **presenting factual material**, not trying to entertain or persuade. This leaves readers free to draw their own conclusions. Informative writing is therefore impersonal and unemotional.

- **Facts** can be verified as accurate and supported by evidence whereas **opinions** are based on thoughts and feelings. For example, 'Ireland is well-known for its writers and poets' (fact). 'Ireland's writers and poets are the best in the entire world' (opinion).

- Information should be presented in a **logical coherent style**, so that it can be easily understood.

- Informative texts (such as encyclopaedias, reports, textbooks, etc.) **expand our knowledge** of the world and have a straightforward style. They often include lots of data and statistics.

NOTE

Although statistics are factual, **they can be used to support different viewpoints**. They can sometimes mislead or deceive people. As Benjamin Disraeli once said: 'There are three kinds of lies – lies, damned lies and statistics'.

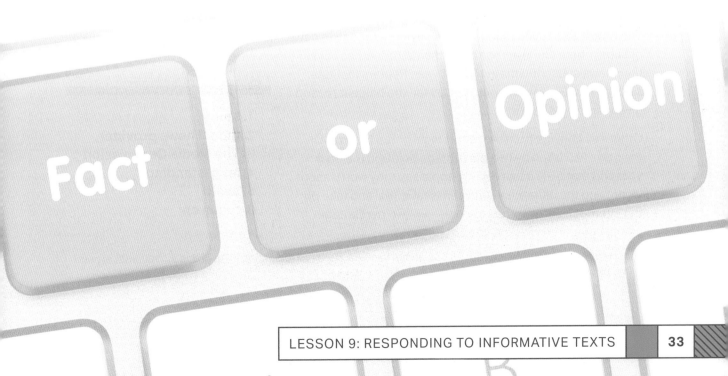

YOUNG PEOPLE'S INTEREST IN NEWS

The text below (from breakingnews.ie) was written in response to a survey which found a sharp decline in Irish young people's interest in news.

Read the text carefully, paying particular attention to the writer's language use.

Younger people's interest in the news has plunged since 2016, according to a survey[1] of more than 2,000 people in Ireland. Just 28% of Irish 18-24 year olds say they are 'extremely' or 'very' interested in the news, down from 53% in 2016. The study was conducted as part of the Reuters[2] Institute for the Study of Journalism's 46-country global digital news report.

The difference between this age group and over-65s, some 69% of whom reported strong interest in the news, 'could not be starker', said DCU's Institute of Future Media, Democracy and Society (FuJo) in its analysis of the report.

Concern about what is real or fake online is also comparatively high in Ireland at 64%, up from 58% last year. Celene Craig, broadcasting commissioner at Coimisiún na Meán[3], said this growing level of concern about online misinformation was one of the 'standout findings' of the Irish report.

The global report also found that more young people are accessing news via TikTok with users tending to pay more attention to celebrities and social media influencers than to journalists or media companies for news. The Chinese-owned app is the 'fastest growing social network' in the global survey – used by 44 per cent of 18-24-year-olds for any purpose and by 20% for news.

The shift comes as the use of Facebook as a news source declines with 28% of surveyed people saying they accessed news via the platform in 2023 compared with 42% in 2016.

Research found that TikTok, Instagram and Snapchat users tend to pay more attention to celebrities and social media influencers than they do to journalists or media companies when it comes to news topics while news organisations on legacy[4] social networks like Facebook and X (formerly Twitter) still attract most attention. News usage for X has remained 'relatively stable' in most countries, according to the report.

Reuters Institute director Rasmus Neilsen said: 'Younger generations increasingly eschew[5] direct discovery for all but the most appealing brand. They have little interest in many conventional news offers oriented towards older generations' habits, interests, and values, and instead embrace the more personality-based, participatory, and personalised options offered by social media, often looking beyond legacy platforms to new entrants (many of whom drive few referrals to media organisations and do not prioritise[6] news).

The report also found that growth in payment for online news has stalled with more than one-third of subscribers (39%) across more than 20 countries saying they have cancelled or renegotiated their news subscriptions in the last year. Reuters Institute said the need to save money was 'by far' the biggest reason given for the cutbacks.

Other key findings from the report highlighted that trust in the news has fallen by two percentage points in the past year and that 56% of surveyed people say they worry about identifying the difference between what is real and fake on the internet when it comes to news – up two percentage points compared with last year.

1. **study**
2. **global news provider**
3. **The Media Commission**
4. **long-standing**
5. **avoid**
6. **focus on**

(Figures are from YouGov Plc with 93,895 adults in 46 countries participating in an online survey, with around 2,000 people per market.)

QUESTION A

(i)   Based on your reading of the text, identify and explain three significant findings which are presented in the survey into Irish young people's interest in news. Support your answer with reference to the text. **(15)**

 Allow about 15 minutes and aim for three focused, supported points in short paragraphs.

SAMPLE ANSWER

1. The most important finding is that young Irish people aren't all that interested in news about current politics. The statistics speak for themselves. Down from 53% to just 28%. I think this is the key figure that comes out of the survey. It's significant because it shows the difference between younger and older people. Most of the newspapers are read by the older generation with an interest in politics.

> First finding – young Irish adults are not interested in news
>
> Significance – difference between older and younger people

2. The above text also includes a key finding in the last paragraph about what is real or fake online. The survey is highlighting that more and more young just people don't believe what they see online which isn't too surprising at all to me. There is no real control on the internet, so all sorts of gossip and half-truth is uploaded as news. It's not true half the time. Take conspiracy theories, for example. In one way, this is a good sign as it shows that the younger generation are thinking more for themselves instead of believing everything they are told.

> Second finding – difference between real or fake
>
> Significance – young people are aware of what is true

3. Another standout finding in the report is to do with how young people pay so much attention to TikTok and Snapchat because they're interested in following media celebrities and influencers. I've read that a lot of kids want to be YouTubers when they finish school. It's not too surprising when you hear about the money that young people can make these days by creating social media content. The survey is very informative because it explains how life is changing through the research that was done.

> Third finding – huge interest in TikTok and Snapchat
>
> Significance – possibility of good jobs in social media

- Focuses well on three findings in the survey, using reference to the text.

- More detailed use of data expected in the second and third paragraphs.

- Some good personal discussion, exploring the significance of the report.

- Points are clearly expressed and language use is functional.

- Overall, a solid response that engages with the text.   **(12/15)**

CLASS/HOMEWORK ACTIVITY

QUESTION A

(iii) Features of informative writing are used effectively in the above text to give a clear and interesting perspective into the decline in Irish young people's interest in news. Discuss this statement, supporting your response with reference to four language features.   **(20)**

🕐 **Allow about 20 minutes to write four focused, supported points in short paragraphs.**

PROMPT

- Is the survey based on reliable research?

- Are the findings presented clearly and coherently?

- To what extent is the style objective and impartial?

- How important is detailed factual material and statistics?

- Is the data in the report verifiable?

- Are readers left to make up their own minds about the survey?

!

10 Visual Literacy

Learning aim: To improve visual literacy and write effectively about visual texts

Visual literacy is the ability to understand, question and find meaning in information presented in the form of images.

Visual texts (such as photographs, book covers, posters, screenshots, graphics, etc.) can be included as part of the Comprehending A question – usually accompanying a written text.

You might be asked to:

● Write a **description of an image** or series of images

● **Analyse an image** and comment on its effectiveness

● **Compare and contrast** the impact of a visual text with a written element.

'READING' VISUAL IMAGES

Consider the purpose of the image.
Is it to inform? Persuade? Entertain? Educate? Shock?

Describe what you see.
Who or what is the subject of the visual?

Note the most striking visual elements.
You might consider setting, details, characters, body language, facial expressions, use of light and shadow, camera angle, etc.

Comment on key visual features.
How important are colours, contrasts and symbols? Are there any surprising details? What do these suggest?

Assess the tone or atmosphere.
Does the image create a particular mood? Does it tell a story or convey a message?

Think about the impact on the viewer.
What is the likely effect of the image?

Write a personal response to this image of an outdoor music festival, commenting on the aspects of the photograph that make the most impact on you. **(15)**

 Allow about 15 minutes and aim for three focused, supported points in short paragraphs.

PROMPT !

- What does the picture show?
- Which details attract your attention?
- What does the body language suggest?
- Does the image inform, surprise, entertain?
- What message does the picture convey?

'READING' A VISUAL TEXT

To 'read' a visual text, you must view the text closely. Work out the main idea and how the **visual codes** help to communicate a message to the audience.

Key techniques (codes) include camera angle, lighting, special effects, layout, dominant image, symbols, patterns, colour, font, graphic, contrast, etc.

Photographers use the camera to construct the **message** they want to communicate. In order to 'read' a photograph, it is important to recognise the techniques that have been used. Visual literacy depends on asking questions as well as analysing images.

Always think about the main purpose of the image. Some photographs can create an emotional response. Others convey meaning and provoke a response. Images can also be **aesthetically pleasing**. These will appeal to our appreciation of beauty or artistic expression.

SAMPLE QUESTION

QUESTION A

(ii) Which of these images do you think best illustrates modern Ireland? You might consider the subject matter, setting, mood, body language, details, props, photographic qualities, etc. **(15)**

🕐 **Allow about 15 minutes and aim for three focused, supported points.**

Image 1

Image 2

Image 3

SAMPLE ANSWER

1. I think the image of Katie Taylor is the one I relate to most. It's not that I'm a big fan of boxing at all, but I admire how Katie Taylor always represents Ireland in such a positive way. Young women especially need good role models who show the qualities that come through in the photo. Not only does it capture a moment when she is after winning a boxing match, but she is proudly wrapped in the Irish flag.

> Choice – Katie Taylor, boxer
>
> Reason – good role model, proud of being Irish

2. The photo conveys Katie's mood of satisfaction after achieving another win in the ring. I think it's actually symbolic of what so many Irish people today can do if they put their talent to good use and work hard. She looks really determined as well and a little emotional as if she knows that she is making people throughout the country very proud of her.

> Shows – Ireland can celebrate its achievements
>
> Evidence – Katie's facial expression

3. One symbol that stands out in this image is the bold colours of the national flag. For such a small country, Ireland is famous all over the world for sport and great writers and actors. Very often, papers publish pictures that give a negative view of Ireland, but this picture is the opposite, clearly showing a talented sportswoman at her best.

> Symbol – bright colours of Irish flag reflect the country's confidence
>
> Effect – shows modern Ireland at its best

EXAMINER'S COMMENT

- Solid, confident response that directly tackles the question.

- Paragraph 1 includes clear points, reasonably supported by apt reference.

- Good attempt to examine visual details, such as body language, colour and symbolism.

- However, a little more developed discussion would have been welcome.

- Expression is functional, but generally well controlled.   **(12/15)**

RESPONDING TO TEXTS THAT HAVE VISUAL ELEMENTS

TOUCHING THE VOID

This text is based on both written and visual elements. The written extract below is from Joe Simpson's book, *Touching the Void*.[1] He and his fellow mountaineer, Simon Yates, successfully climbed Siula Grande Mountain in the Peruvian Andes in 1985. However, during the descent, Simpson broke his leg. Convinced that Joe was dead, Simon cut the rope that joined them together and Joe fell into a crevasse.[2]

Read the following extract carefully, paying particular attention to the writer's language use.

I glanced at the rope stretched tautly[3] above me. It ran up the wall and disappeared onto the slope above. There was no possibility of getting back to that slope some twenty feet above me. I looked at the wall of the crevasse close by my shoulder. On the other side another wall of ice towered

up ten feet away. I was hanging in a shaft of water ice. The decision to look down came as I was in the process of turning. I swung round quickly, catching my smashed knee on the ice wall and howling in a frenzy of pain and fright.

Instead of seeing the rope twisting loosely in a void beneath me, I stared blankly at the snow below my feet, not fully

believing what I was seeing. A floor! There was a wide snow-covered floor fifteen feet below me. There was no emptiness, and no black void. I swore softly, and heard it whisper off the walls around me. Then I let out a cry of delight and relief which boomed round the crevasse. I yelled again and again, listening to the echoes, and laughed between the yells. I was at the bottom of the crevasse.

When I recovered my wits[4] I looked more carefully at the carpet of snow above which I was dangling. My jubilation was quickly tempered when I spotted dark menacing holes in the surface. It wasn't a floor after all. The crevasse opened up into a pear-shaped dome, its sides curving away from me to a width of fifty feet before narrowing again. The snow floor cut through the flat end of this cavern, while the walls above me tapered in to form the thin end of the pear barely ten feet across and nearly 100 feet high. Small fragments of crusty snow patterned down from the roof.

I looked round the enclosed vault[5] of snow and ice, familiarising myself with its shape and size. The walls opposite closed in but didn't meet. A narrow gap had been filled with snow from above to form a cone which rose all the way to the roof. It was about fifteen feet wide at the base and as little as four or five feet across the top.

A pillar of gold light beamed diagonally[6] from a small hole in the roof, spraying bright reflections off the far wall of the crevasse. I was mesmerised by this beam and sunlight burning through the vaulted ceiling from the real world outside. It had me so fixated[7] that I forgot about the uncertain floor below and let myself slide down the rest of the rope. I was going to reach that sunbeam. I knew it then with absolute certainty. How I would do it, and when I would reach it were not considered. I just knew.

1. **nothingness**
2. **crack, opening**
3. **tightly**
4. **senses**
5. **enclosed space**
6. **at an angle**
7. **fascinated**

CLASS/HOMEWORK ACTIVITY

QUESTION A

(i) Based on your reading of the above text (written extract and image), explain three insights you gain into the experience of mountaineering. Support your answer with reference to both the written and visual elements of the text (though not necessarily equally).   **(15)**

🕐 **Allow about 15 minutes and aim for three focused, supported points.**

PROMPT !

- What is the appeal of mountaineering?
- How important is the adventure, risk and danger?
- Do climbers gain strength to face life's other challenges?
- Does teamwork play a big part in mountain climbing?
- To what extent is mountaineering a man's world?

Learning aim: To analyse key features of autobiographical writing

- Autobiographies and memoirs are **very similar** non-fiction genres.

- An autobiography is usually a factual account of **one's own life**.

- Memoirs are non-fiction narratives in which authors **share detailed memories**.

- Autobiographies **highlight key events** in a person's life. They can be used to reflect on challenges, achievements and disappointments.

KEY FEATURES OF AUTOBIOGRAPHICAL WRITING

○ **Personal record of thoughts and feelings** ○ **Written in the first person** ○ **Describes people and places in detail** ○ **Includes a reflective tone** ○ **Readers gain insights into the writer's character**

NOTE

A **biography** is an account of someone's life written by another person. When someone writes their own life story, it's called an **autobiography** ('auto' means 'self').

TEENAGE MEMOIR

The following text is from *One Two Three Four: The Beatles in Time* by Craig Brown. In this extract, Mary Wood remembers being infatuated with one of one of the band members, Paul McCartney.

Read the following extract carefully, paying particular attention to the writer's style.

My father was a doctor, a GP. My dream was that Paul, somehow, would have a minor injury and would have to call at our house for my father to stitch it up. My father would decree[1] it would be best if he went to bed for a couple of days to recover, and since he would be recognised if he went to a hotel, he should stay in our house, in a pop-up hospital ward for one. I would help to nurse him. So then it would only be a matter of time before we got engaged.

The trouble was that Paul didn't come to Northern Ireland very often. But in November 1964 he came and my Aunt Sheila bought tickets for me and my sister and our cousins and we went to the King's Hall in Belfast. The four Beatles came onstage and they held their instruments but any tunes would have been totally drowned out by the mass hysteria of the audience. The hall erupted into screaming and moaning. I just mimed screaming, to fit in. Have you tried screaming? It's not at all easy to do for more than two ten-second bursts. You don't get anywhere and it just wears out your voice. You should try it. We couldn't hear a word anyway, and I don't know if the Beatles were even bothering to play or just miming.

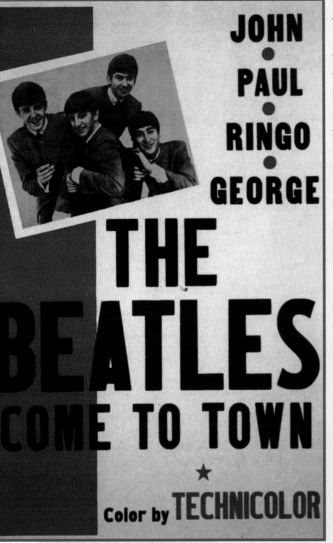

One thing put me off Paul, though. He was pouring with sweat and he wiped the sweat on his clothes. Despite this I genuinely, at the back of my mind, thought I was going to marry him. I felt it in every fibre[2] of my being. It was the reason I didn't work for my A-Levels. I reckoned that anyway I wouldn't have time to go to university or have a career as I would be constantly on tour with Paul. The fact that I was going to marry Paul informed my behaviour in general, but I didn't tell anyone, obviously, because it was a kind of religious thing, a secret between me and God.

The day I turned eighteen I got on a plane to London. I had left school and done my A-Levels. I got bad grades. I knew Paul lived in St John's Wood, so I went to the nearest tube station. I thought it would require some sleuthing,[3] but no, the man behind the counter of the tube station told me the exact address, and, armed with an *A to Z*,[4] I walked towards it.

I had imagined that I would just stand outside his house and sooner or later Paul would come out and, seeing me, invite me in, and then he would fall in love with me and the engagement would be announced within a few days and that would show my parents that I knew best about my life plans. That would put them in their place.

1. **order**
2. **part**
3. **detective work**
4. **street map**
5. **friendship**
6. **dreamy**

But when I got to the house I was amazed that there were about twenty to thirty other girls there. How come there was a sense of camaraderie[5] when we were all competing for the same prize? I don't know. Perhaps it was part of that moony[6] adolescent thing, and we didn't actually want to set up home with Paul, we were just in love with the idea of it.

The other girls said that Paul wasn't even inside the house anyway. So why were they standing outside crying and moaning and pushing letters through the railings? I think there were railings.

Close analysis of language use in the text is essential for answering questions successfully. The following discussion notes focus on key words and phrases that illustrate the writer's autobiographical writing skill.

- **First-person narrative** and written in the past tense ('My father was a doctor').

- The opening paragraph highlights Mary's **naïve 'dream'** of meeting her idol. She imagines Paul having a 'minor injury', helping to 'nurse him' – and instant romance.

- Vivid **descriptive details** (e.g. 'He wiped the sweat on his clothes.', 'Paul wasn't even inside the house.') and use of dates ('November 1964') showing when events happened help to **make the memoir realistic.**

- Mary's reaction to the Beatles onstage – 'I just mimed screaming.' – reveals her lack of confidence and **need 'to fit in'.**

- The writer's honest observations as an adult add a **reflective quality**: 'I don't know if the Beatles were even bothering to play.', 'Perhaps it was part of that moony adolescent thing.', 'We were just in love with the idea.'.

- The extract focuses on youthful innocence and **coming-of-age,** giving readers a good sense of Mary's impressionable character.

SAMPLE QUESTION

QUESTION A

(i) Based on your reading of the extract, choose three observations Mary makes and explain what each observation reveals about her character. Support your answer with reference to the text.

(15)

SAMPLE ANSWER

1. Mary Wood was a very funny character as a teenager even though she wasn't too keyed in to the real world. She is very young and fancies her idol, Paul. She says 'I was going to marry him'. This just goes to prove how immature she was. But she keeps her plans to herself because she is unsure about what she hopes for and lives in a sort of fantasy world and daydreams about a famous popstar.

> First observation – she idolised Paul
>
> Revelation – young girl's immaturity

2. Another thing Mary observes is a sign of just how foolish she is in thinking she will be married to a celebrity and globe-trotting all the time. She says 'It was the reason I didn't work for my A-Levels'. This reveals an immature attitude to studying and exams, in my opinion.

> Second observation – romantic idea of marrying a pop idol
>
> Revelation – childish attitude to life

3. My third observation from Mary is about challenging her parents about getting engaged, 'That would put them in their place'. She is probably an average rebel teenager who likes to have a go against her own parents. Just because she left home at eighteen and had went to London and married a rich celeb – in her own mind, so to speak. I thought she is funny in ways but just an ordinary rebel teenager.

> Third observation –
> challenges parents
>
> Revelation – typically
> rebellious young person

EXAMINER'S COMMENT

- Reasonably focused response to the question.
- Identified three observations and commented briefly on each one.
- More developed discussion would have raised the standard.
- Repetition and some awkward expression, e.g. in the final paragraph.
- Good overall sense of the writer's youthful immaturity. **(10/15)**

CLASS/HOMEWORK ACTIVITY

QUESTION A

(ii)   In the extract on the previous page, Mary Wood recalls a time during her teenage years when her hopes and dreams ended in disappointment. To what extent can you relate to Mary's experience?

🕐 **Allow about 15 minutes and aim to write three focused points.**

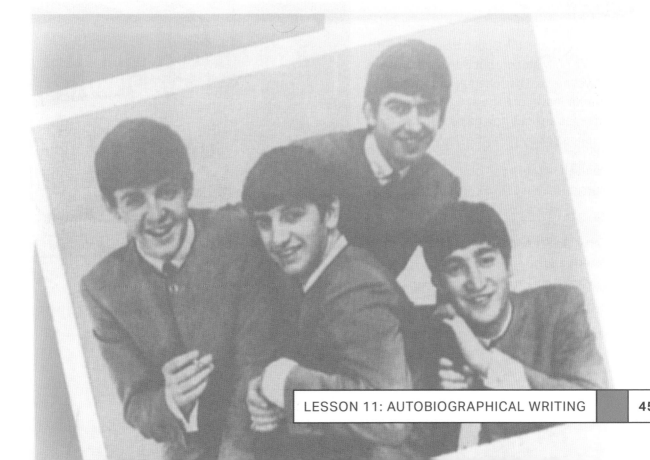

A CRUELTY

In this extract from *A Cruelty* by Kevin Barry, the story's central character is making his daily train journey from Boyle, his hometown, to Sligo.

Read the following extract carefully, paying particular attention to the writer's use of language.

He climbs the twenty-three steps of the metal traverse[1] bridge at 9.25 a.m., and not an instant before. Boyle station, a grey and blowy summer's day. He counts each step as he climbs, the ancient rusted girders of the bridge clamped secure with enormous bolts, and the way the roll of his step is a fast plimsoll shuffle as he crosses – the stride is determined, the arms are swinging – and he counts off the twenty-three steps that descend again to the far-side platform. The clanky bamp of the last metal step gives way to a softer footfall on the platform's smooth aged stone, and the surge of the Dublin–Sligo train comes distantly, but now closer, and now at a great building roar along the track – the satisfaction of timing it just right – and the train's hot breeze unsettles his hair. The train eases to a halt, and his hair fixes; the doors beep three times and airily hiss open: an expectant gasp. He takes his usual place in carriage A. There is no question of a ticket being needed but the inspector sticks his head into the carriage anyway to bid a good morning.

'That's not a bad-looking day at all,' Donie says.

It is his joke to say this in all weathers. He said it throughout the great freeze of Christmas and the year's turn, he said it during the floods of November '09. Now a roar comes out of the north, also, and the Sligo–Dublin train pulls in alongside, and its noise deflates,[2] with the passengers boredly staring – it is at Boyle station always that the trains keep company, for a few minutes, and for Donie this is a matter of pride. Boyle is a town happily fated, he believes, a place where things of interest will tend to happen.

The beeps and the hissing, the carriages are sealed, and the Dublin train heads off for Connolly station, but Donie's train does not yet move. The schedule declares his train will leave for Sligo at 9.33 a.m. and he becomes anxious now as he watches the seconds tick by on his Casio watch.

9.33.35

9.33.36

9.33.37

And when the seconds ascend into the fifties, his breath starts to come in hard panicked stabs of anxiety, and he speaks.

'We'd want to be making a move here, lads,' he says.

It is a painful twenty-eight seconds into 9.34 a.m. when the train drags up its great power from within, and the doors close again and the departure is made.

Why, Donie demands, when the train has had a full eight minutes to wait on the platform, can it not leave precisely at the appointed time of its schedule?

'There is no call for it,' he says.

And it is not as if his watch is out–no fear–for he checks it each morning against the speaking clock. The speaking clock is a state-run service; it surely cannot be wrong. If it was, the whole system would be thrown out.

The train climbs to the high ground outside Boyle. He rides the ascent into the Curlew Mountains, and he whistles past the graveyard. The judder and surge of the engine is its usual excitement and he tries to forget the anxiety of Boyle station, but it recedes[3] slowly as tide. Now the broken-down stone walls of the old rising fields. Now the mournful cows still wet from the dew and night's drizzle. Now the greenish tone of the galvanised tin roof on the lost shack. The spits of rain against the window, and the high looming of the Bricklieves[4] on a mid-distant rise, north-westerly, a smooth-cut limestone plateau.[5]

He was allowed to make the journey first on the morning of his sixteenth birthday. This is now the twentieth year of his riding the Boyle–Sligo leg, all the working days of the week, all the weeks of the year. It is Donie's belief that if he is not on the 9.33 train, the 9.33 will not run, and who is there to say otherwise.

1. **cross**
2. **decreases**
3. **fades from view**
4. **Co. Sligo hills**
5. **flat upland scenery**

SAMPLE QUESTION

QUESTION A – 50 MARKS

(i) Based on your reading of the above text, explain three insights you gain into Donie's thoughts and feelings which help to reveal his character. You may address thoughts and feelings separately or together. **(15)**

🕐 **Allow about 15 minutes and aim for three focused, supported points.**

SAMPLE ANSWER

1. Donie seems to me like a very strange character who's completely obsessed with counting and thinking all the time about time-keeping, for example, he 'counts each step' at the train station. He is used to the train being exactly on time and this makes him feel good. He gets a great 'satisfaction of timing it just right'. This gives me a definite insight into his thoughts and feelings.

> First insight – obsessive character
>
> Reveals – Donie's love of routine

2. Donie is also a man of habit who doesn't change his routine, for example, he always picks his 'usual place' in the carriage. He also makes the same joke about the weather every morning. But if the train is late, Donie isn't really able to cope. He has a fear of things not going exactly to plan. A good example of this is when his train is just a few minutes late and he gets really edgy and has 'stabs of anxiety'.

> Second insight – a man of habit
>
> Reveals – his inability to cope if anything goes wrong

3. Another insight into how Donie's mind works is at the end of this text when the train gets going and he is back in his normal routine. This is when Donie relaxes again and feels better. He is a lot more at ease looking out at the countryside. He is really only able to be calm when everything goes perfectly. I see Donie as a very insecure man in that any unexpected upset or change completely upsets his thoughts and feelings.

> Third insight – need for perfection in order to relax
>
> Reveals – Donie's insecurity

EXAMINER'S COMMENT

- Solid, sustained and focused response to the question.

- Commented on three insights of the character's thoughts and feelings.

- Some good use of supportive textual reference.

- More developed discussion of Donie's personality would have improved the answer.

- Expression is generally clear and functional, but slightly repetitive throughout. **(11/15)**

CLASS/HOMEWORK ACTIVITY

The questions below follow on from the sample question on the previous page. Try them in the classroom or as homework.

(ii) Describe a time when you had to deal with feeling particularly stressed and under pressure. Explain the situation that developed and your response to it. **(15)**

🕐 **Allow about 15 minutes and aim for three focused, supported points**

(iii) Features of both narrative writing and descriptive writing are used effectively by Kevin Barry to engage the reader in Donie's world. Discuss this statement, supporting your response with reference to four language features in the text. You may include features of narrative writing, features of descriptive writing, or both in your discussion. **(20)**

🕐 **Allow about 20 minutes and aim for four focused, supported points.**

PROMPT

- Does the compelling narrative help to create empathy with Donie?

- Are details used effectively to create a sense of an extraordinary character?

- Does the imagery reveal a dark vision of the world: 'unsettles', 'stabs', etc.?

- Is Donie's journey symbolic? What does it suggest?

- Impact of tension, changing moods, inner conflict, the character's vulnerability.

- Effect of the dramatic setting, poetic imagery, repetition, hypnotic rhythms, etc.

!

COMPREHENDING B OVERVIEW

The Comprehending B section (worth 50 marks) is often referred to as **'functional writing'**, which is writing for a specific purpose.

You are likely to use a **particular format**, e.g. a talk, letter, email, diary, blog, opinion piece, speech, introduction, report, review, etc.

For each Comprehending B task, it is essential to use the **appropriate register** (language, tone and layout).

Aim for around **450 words** (usually four or five paragraphs written over 40 minutes).

NOTE

Comprehending B functional writing questions ask you to **write for a particular, practical reason**.

Study the wording of the question closely to identify the various elements or aspects that need to be addressed.

PCLM MARKING SCHEME

Comprehending B questions are marked using the State Examination Commission **PCLM marking scheme**.

This refers to: Purpose, Coherence, Language and Mechanics. **(Total: 50 marks)**

Purpose: Are all aspects of the task being addressed? **(15 marks)**

Coherence: Is the response controlled, paragraphed and sustained? **(15 marks)**

Language: Is the writing appropriate to the task (tone, fluency, punctuation)? **(15 marks)**

Mechanics: Are spellings and grammar accurate? **(5 marks)**

To understand Comprehending B questions, focus on:

- **What** do I have to write about? (**content**)
- **Who** am I as writer/speaker? (**persona**)
- **For whom** am I writing? (**audience**)
- **Why** am I writing this? (**purpose**)
- **What type** of language and tone will I use? (**register**)
- **What format** should the writing take? (**layout**)

Learning aim: To understand the key elements of an effective talk

Comprehending Question B tasks frequently include writing the text of a short talk or presentation. It's important to get **the right register (tone) to suit the occasion**.

The register of a talk refers to the **choice of language** and **speaking style**.

An appropriate register or tone will be suggested by the following:

● What is the point of this talk? (**purpose**)

● Who is the speaker? (**persona**)

● Who is being addressed? (**audience**)

What is the **purpose of the talk?** Is it meant to be informative, personal, entertaining, reflective, persuasive or descriptive? Or perhaps a mix of some of these?

You might be asked, for example, to write the text of a short talk to be given to your school year group about **a controversial issue**, such as the use of mobile phones by students during school hours.

Discursive language considering a variety of arguments or viewpoints may be suitable in this case. Or you could feel very strongly about the subject and deliver a more **emotive**, **persuasive** speech.

A much more informal register will be appropriate in a short talk welcoming a well-known celebrity to your school. The **tone is likely to be relaxed, humorous and complimentary** as you will be focusing positively on your guest's achievements and influence.

NOTE

Some talks are formal and serious.

Others are casual and conversational.

SAMPLE QUESTION B (TALK)

QUESTION B – 50 MARKS

As a member of the Student Council, you have agreed to give a talk at a school function to mark the retirement of your principal after six years in the role. In addition to expressing your own personal tribute, you should outline some of the changes that have taken place over that time, and highlight the principal's impact on both the school and local community. Write the text of the talk you would deliver.

 Allow about 40 minutes and aim for around 450 words.

PLANNING YOUR RESPONSE

Planning is essential to producing a successful response. **Study the wording** of the question closely to understand the task.

Ask yourself the following:

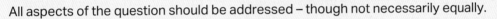

1   What are the main elements of the task I have to address?

- Write the text of **a talk giving a personal tribute** to your retiring principal.

- Outline some key **changes** that have taken place.

- Highlight the principal's **impact on school** and **local community**.

All aspects of the question should be addressed – though not necessarily equally.

2   Who am I as the writer? A Leaving Cert student.

3   Who is my target audience? School community.

4   What type of language will I use? Informative, personal, reflective, anecdotal, etc.

HOW DO I STRUCTURE (ORGANISE) MY RESPONSE?

- Brief introduction and personal tribute.

- Address other key elements of the task.

- Brief conclusion.

SAMPLE ANSWER

1. Good afternoon, everybody. It's such a pleasure to be speaking to you all on this really important day. I can't actually believe it's almost six years since Mrs Rice became principal. It seems like the distant past totally when my classmates and I were nervous little first years. Hard to believe looking at you now, I know.

> Introduction establishes the talk register and addresses the task.

2. At our very first assembly, Mrs Rice said she had a small secret to share. This seemed a bit strange as we were ready to hear another lecture about studying 24/7 for the dreaded Junior Cycle. But what Mrs Rice told us was that she herself was feeling very nervous as it was also her first week as principal. What I still remember most is her saying she hoped we would always be good friends and that we would look out for one another.

> Personal memories reflect the affectionate tone.
>
> Expression weakened at times by repetition.

3. I admit I don't think I really knew it then, but that was an important moment. And like so many students here who appreciate Mrs Rice's helpfulness, it just summed up her helpful character. She has been an amazing principal. As you all know, Mrs Rice (or Mrs R as she is better known) is a really kind person who treats everyone fairly and respectfully. She isn't a pushover either. But she takes time to listen to students and really treats people fairly. She tells you the truth if you're out of line, but always explains the reasons for her decisions.

4. School life has changed so much and our principal has really made a fantastic impact at keeping up with the times. Every September, there's been changes to help our education. During Mrs Rice's time, we have seen new I.T. and Science rooms and brilliant library facilities as well as the extended playing fields. Not to mention my own all-time fave, the sixth year recreation room oasis. Remember, what happens inside the recreation rooms stays inside the recreation room!

5. Thanks to our principal, there's a great sense of respect throughout the school, within classes, during after-school activities, between students, between staff and students. And that sense of courtesy comes from the top. It was there from the start and it's what makes the school a very happy place.

6. Mrs Rice also involves the local community. For example, the 5K School Run fund-raiser at Easter and the Christmas concert. Local people also take part in the Halloween Arts Week.

> More development expected on this key element of the question.

7. Mrs Rice, I think you know how respected you are and how the school community will really miss you. I just can't thank you enough for all that you have done. But speaking for every one of us here, enjoy every moment of your retirement. And can I end by saying that you really have looked out for us all as you promised. So thank you so much from all of us.

> Talk rounded off effectively on a note of sincere respect and appreciation.

(470 words)

GRADE: H1

P =   14/15
C =   13/15
L =   13/15
M =   5/5

TOTAL = 45/50

EXAMINER'S COMMENT

- Overall, a successful top-grade response.
- Well-organised talk addresses three key of the key elements (personal tribute, changes, impact on the school) very well.
- More focus on the fourth element (local community) would be expected in paragraph 6.
- The relaxed but reflective personal tone is appropriate and there is a clear sense of engagement with the audience ('like so many students here', 'everyone here', etc.).
- Language has the right register for a student tribute.
- Expression is clear – apart from some repetition in paragraph 3.
- Talk rounded off well with a flashback reference to paragraph 2.

WRITING A GOOD OPENING PARAGRAPH

An effective **opening paragraph** will:

 Engage your audience

 Let them know **what to expect**

> *If I could just say a few words ... I'd be a better public speaker.*
>
> **Homer Simpson**

NOTE

The **first sentence** should hook the listener. An interesting quote, one-liner, definition or curious fact can often be effective. A short, dramatic question can also succeed in getting attention.

CLASS/HOMEWORK ACTIVITY

Write the opening paragraph of a short talk to your school year group about the meaning and importance of friendship and loyalty.

Aim for around 120 words.

PROMPT !

Briefly introduce your views on friendship, considering some of the following points:

- Do reliable friends improve one's sense of self-worth?
- Importance of emotional support in coping with everyday challenges?
- Can friends offer different perspectives on life?
- Dangers of peer pressure, exploitation, dependency?

Friendship

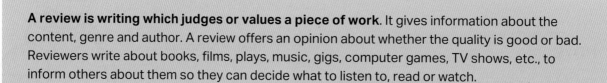

Learning aim: To write an effective review

A review is writing which judges or values a piece of work. It gives information about the content, genre and author. A review offers an opinion about whether the quality is good or bad. Reviewers write about books, films, plays, music, gigs, computer games, TV shows, etc., to inform others about them so they can decide what to listen to, read or watch.

A review should usually have the following sections:

Introduction

The **introduction** contains **basic information** about what is being reviewed. This is likely to include title, genre and the names of those involved in the work is given.

Description

The **description** gives **details** about the work which might be of interest to readers. If it is a film, play or novel, give a brief outline of the story, but do not give away the ending or any important twists in the plot.

NOTE

When writing a review, always keep your **target readers** in mind. Are they teenagers or older adults? Or are you writing for a general audience? What is likely to **interest** your readers? Remember to use **suitable language** that they will understand.

Evaluation

The **evaluation** is the reviewer's **opinion and judgement** of the work. For films or TV shows, consider the plot, main character/s, acting, setting, special effects and direction.

Recommendation

The **recommendation** is the reviewer's personal advice. Was the album worth listening to? Was the gig worth the money? Was the book worth reading? Suggest the type of viewer/listener/reader who might enjoy it.

SAMPLE QUESTION B (REVIEW)

You have been invited to contribute a review of a film you saw recently for the series in your school magazine entitled, 'It's Worth the Watch'. The series will describe the genre and plot of the film, highlighting positive and negative aspects, and arguing whether or not you believe this film is worth the watch.

PLANNING YOUR RESPONSE

Planning is essential to producing a successful response. **Study the wording** of the question closely to understand the task.

Ask yourself the following:

● What are the main elements or the task I have to address?

Write a **film review** describing **genre and outlining plot, highlighting positive and negative aspects.**

Four aspects in total:

1   Who am I as the writer? A Leaving Cert student.

2   Who is my target audience? School community.

3   What type of language will I use? Informative, personal, persuasive, etc.

4   How do I structure (organise) my response?

    ● Brief introduction, outlining genre and plot.

    ● Address the main elements of the task (though not necessarily equally).

    ● Brief conclusion.

SAMPLE ANSWER

1. Oppenheimer is a 3-hour biopic, a biographical thriller film. It is directed by Christopher Nolan, famous for the science fiction film, Inception. The new film is about the American scientist, J. Robert Oppenheimer. He had an important part developing the atomic bomb.

> **Introduction**
>
> Basic information – film title, director, genre, plot overview

2. The film includes three different time periods. This is a well-known technique of this director. The story is divided into sections covering Oppenheimer's studies in the 1920s. It then deals with his work on the secret Manhattan Project developing the bomb during World War 2. The third part deals his security hearing in 1954 when Oppenheimer was investigated about whether his work could continue.

3. The director is focused on Oppenheimer's complicated character throughout. Cillian Murphy, a favourite actor of Nolan's, is brilliant as the nervous, chain-smoking scientist. Not only does he capture the personality of the troubled genius, he also looks very like him.

> **Description**
>
> Details about the film – leading actors and their portrayal of key characters

4. There's also a strong cast in the film. Oppenheimer's bitter wife is beautifully played by Emily Blunt. Their secret signal if the bomb testing is sucessful is 'Bring in the laundry'. Florence Pugh plays the member of the american communist party, Jean Tatlock, who had an affair with Oppenheimer.

5. Nolan uses very little CGI (or computer generated imagery). Instead, real explosives were used to film the nuclear test. I found this scene both beautiful and horrifying. It is the climax of the film. The loud thumping music sometimes drowns out the dialogue, but this adds to the tense atmosphere. Colour is used very well to show the story from a personal point of view. White and black, particularly in the last section of the film, shows the story from a viewpoint that is more based on history.

> Interesting aspects of the film – special effects, music, colour

6. I think the film would have been perfect if it had ended with the explosion of the 'Trinity' bomb which was the first time an atomic bomb was tested, however, another hour in black and white is added on to look at Oppenheimer's security hearing. I imagine lots of people loosing interest.

> Negative aspect
>
> The last hour drags

7. I feel this film is worth the watch particularly for the people that like history and are interested in World War 2 or the character of Oppenheimer as a troubled genius. Nolan is sucessful in showing what it would have been like to be Oppenheimer. The plot shows Oppenheimer's response to what happened as a result of his actions. The scientist is shown as a hero, yet Nolan places a nightmare vision of the victims of the bomb beside the admiration.

> Recommendation
>
> Why the film is worth watching and who it will appeal to

8. The director leaves the audience to think about whether Oppenheimer was right that this bomb 'will end all wars'. Should the USA have nuked Hiroshima and Nagasaki? I would rate this film 9/10.

(450 words)

EXAMINER'S COMMENT

GRADE: H2

P = 13/15
C = 12/15
L = 11/15
M = 4/5

TOTAL = 40/50

- Solid review that addresses the task reasonably well throughout.
- Includes some useful background information (e.g. in paragraphs 2 and 5).
- More emphasis on targeting the likely interests of a second-level student audience needed.
- Interesting points in paragraph 7 deserve further development.
- Expression is functional but slightly repetitive and lacking freshness.
- Some mechanical errors ('sucessful'; 'american', 'loosing', 'people that').

CLASS/HOMEWORK ACTIVITY

Write a paragraph for inclusion in an article on your school website in which you recommend one movie that made a lasting impression on you

Aim for around 120 words.

PROMPT !

- How do you explain the long-term effect of the movie?
- Which aspects of the film made the most impact? Plot? Theme? Acting?
- What is your main reason for recommending it?
- Is your review informative? Descriptive? Persuasive? Or a mix of these?

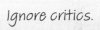

Ignore critics.

Anne Rice

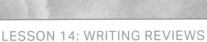

WHAT IS A FEATURE ARTICLE?

● A feature article or opinion piece is a **written prose piece** which usually appears in print media (newspapers, magazines, etc.) or on a website.

● These pieces usually **focus on people or issues** rather than events and are written by journalists, freelance writers and bloggers.

● Feature articles can **inform, entertain and persuade**.

● They offer a **reflective, personal (and sometimes humorous) viewpoint** on life.

In responding to Comprehending B questions, your writing style will depend on the purpose of your article. Many reflective pieces include descriptive and informative language, but there will often be elements of persuasive and narrative writing.

Articles are often autobiographical or deal with issues in the news. However, you may be asked to write to write about any subject, such as:

● School
● Hobbies
● Sport

● Social issues
● Modern-day life
● Work

● The arts
● Celebrity and media
● Plans for the future, etc.

SOME STYLISTIC QUALITIES OF ARTICLES

○ **Reflective approach to the topic**
○ **Personal engaging tone**
○ **Lively anecdotes or illustrations**
○ **Humorous touches**
○ **Conversational and emotive language**
○ **Short paragraphs and sentences**

THINGS YOUR MAM TOLD YOU WHEN YOU WERE YOUNGER THAT YOU WISH YOU'D LISTENED TO NOW

She was right all along.

AS THE YEARS roll by, I often remember things my mother told me when I was younger that, if I had listened, would have prevented me from landing in certain situations I wish I hadn't.

At the time, my mam's nuggets of wisdom felt like demands, constraints around the free and independent person I wanted to be.

But looking back, what are the main pieces of advice we wished we'd listened to, the truly frustrating things that have happened as a result, and the ways we can make it right this time round.

'SCHOOL YEARS ARE THE BEST YEARS OF YOUR LIFE'

How many times were we told to 'enjoy them, they won't last forever' before rolling our eyes, putting on our Dubarrys, and going to school in a huff?

Can you imagine it now?

Finishing every day by 3.30pm, getting two breaks throughout the day, midterms, summer *and* Christmas holidays, and all the while sat having a laugh with your best friends?

We didn't appreciate it then, but we'd sure as hell appreciate it now, just like our mam said …

'DON'T SIT SO CLOSE TO THE SCREEN'

Curtains closed, pyjamas still on, cushions on the floor, sitting two feet from the telly watching 'Satitude'. Yes, this is what a lot of Saturdays looked like when we were small.

Our mams would yell and scream to open the curtains, go outside and enjoy the fresh air, but at the very least, not to sit so close to the telly.

Fast forward to present day and many of us now rely on glasses to see our screens or get stress headaches from looking at them all because of decades of bad habits.

'DON'T BITE YOUR NAILS'

In our defence, we knew this was good advice the first time we heard it.

But over the years, we got used to our hands being slapped away from our mouths, getting scolding looks when we thought we were taking a sneaky nibble and just generally being reminded that it's a disgusting habit.

'LEAVE YOUR HAIR ALONE'

From ironing it flat, straightening it daily to colouring it with dodgy box dyes we're still trying to grow out, our mams warned us repeatedly to stay well clear and embrace our natural hair.

The curls you hated were something they said others would 'die for'. The red hue you wanted to hide beneath blonde highlights was something they said made you 'unique'.

Every hair decision was met with an opposing argument.

'YOU'LL HAVE PLENTY OF TIME FOR BOYFRIENDS'

Whether you were in a relationship or not, or whether you were looking for one or not, your mam would often remind you that you have plenty of time for boyfriends.

Early on, it felt like a warning away from mingling with boys in general, but later on, it felt more like an encouragement to enjoy being on our own and learning who we were.

'YOU'LL THANK ME ONE DAY'

Years on, whether it was big things or small, we've grown grateful to our mothers in a way that is much deeper than when we were younger.

Rather than being grateful for the spins they gave us, the pocket money, or letting us go out with friends, we've grown grateful for the time they gave us.

Time spent allowing us to do the things we loved, helping us to learn to embrace the things we didn't, and sacrificing any spare minute to share advice and guidance to help us through the rest.

The list of things to thank them for is endless, a task nobody could complete in one lifetime.

So now instead, *we* make the sweeping statement, hoping it's enough.

Mam – for everything, thank you.

Author: Orlaith Condon

Adapted from 'Things your mam told you when you were younger that you wish you'd listened to', dailyedge.ie

Close study of the language used by Orlaith Condon provides useful tips on writing effective opinion pieces.

- The article's catchy heading is lively and light-hearted – and the writer's tone is personal and affectionate. This is a good way of **attracting the interest of readers** and get them thinking about their own experiences of growing up.

- Most of the article is based on Orlaith Condon's **warm memories** of her 'mam' and the unwanted advice and warnings she recalls.

- There is **good use of anecdotes** (short personal stories) to keep readers interested. Humorous details add to their appeal.

- The writer looks back on her early experiences with **nostalgia** (a longing for the past). Readers are also likely to feel sentimental about childhood.

- The **detailed description** (e.g. 'sitting two feet from the telly') and vivid images (e.g. 'taking a sneaky nibble') bring family scenes to life.

- Paragraphs are short and the **language is straightforward** throughout.

- **Sub-headings** outline the key idea in each paragraph and break up the text, making it easier to read.

- The strong **conclusion is emotive** and rounds off the article in a way that most readers will relate to.

CLASS/HOMEWORK ACTIVITY

Based on your reading of Orlaith Condon's article, what main point (or points) is the writer making about her experience of growing up and the way she now feels? Support your answer with reference to the text.

Aim for around 120 words.

- Is the key point that people's understanding changes as they get older?

- Or is the key point that the past is usually a good source of humour?

- Is the author making any serious points or simply wallowing in sentimentality?

> A **strong article** changes minds.
> A **weak article** falls flat.

Learning aim: To write engaging feature articles

- A feature article presents **information** in a creative, descriptive way.
- It's important to use **the right register** of a feature article.
- This means **writing appropriately** to suit your purpose and the audience.

When planning your article, ask yourself:

- What key point do I want to make?
- Who am I as a writer?
- Who are my readers?
- What type of language and tone will I use?

GET OFF TO A GOOD START

- Begin with a **strong statement or question** to make your readers stay for the answer.
- Present a **surprising fact**. Let them know they will learn something new in this article.
- **Keep it brief**. Short paragraphs and short sentences encourage a quick reading pace.
- Use bullet points or headings to **break up the text**. Many readers skim blog articles.
- The ending of an effective article should **emphasise your main point** and draw the article to a close.

SAMPLE ARTICLE

You have been invited to write an article entitled 'In Praise of Fast Food' to appear on your school blog. In your article you should: explain what you know about the tradition or history of fast food, reflect on your own earliest experiences of eating in fast food outlets, discuss some of the main fast food benefits, and give your views on why fast food will be more popular than ever in the future.

PLANNING YOUR RESPONSE

Planning is essential to producing a successful response. **Study the wording** of the question closely to understand the task.

Ask yourself the following:

1   What are the main elements of the task I have to address?

2   Who am I as the writer? A Leaving Cert student.

3   Who is my target audience? School community.

4   What type of language will I use? Descriptive, informative, personal, reflective, anecdotal, etc.

Identify the key elements of the question:

- Outline what you know about the **history** of fast food
- Reflect on your **early experiences** of fast food outlets
- Discuss some fast food **benefits**
- Explain why fast food will **continue to be popular**

(All four aspects should be addressed – though not necessarily equally)

SAMPLE ANSWER

IN PRAISE OF FAST FOOD

1. Fast food! Why do those two words sometimes raise depressing images of overweight people and heart attacks? Well, today I would like to present a much more positive picture. I will explore the benefits of fast food, its traditions, my early experiences of eating fast food and how fast food is going to continue to be popular. Fast food is not necessarily junk food!

> Opening addresses the question and presents a clear viewpoint.

2. Fast food is mass-produced food. It is prepared and served quickly to large numbers of commuters, travelers and shift workers. I found out the word was first used around 1950 for those who were hungry, in a hurry and with a small amount of money to spend. Would you believe that the fast-food industry is worth 570 billion globally? Obviously, there is a great demand for this service!

> Range of illustrations from history adds interest.

3. Looking back on history, people lived in tiny appartments which had little space for cooking and storing food. Just like today, I've also read that way back 2,000 years ago, a popular snack from street sellers in Rome was bread soaked in wine. In London and Paris, street fast food was mostly meat pies and pasties. Just like today's fast food, it was conviently wrapped in pastry and very easy to carry.

> Personal anecdote might have been developed to argue for the social impact of fast food outlets.

4. One of the best things about visiting other countries is sampling the local fast food. In West Africa, the roadside stands sell char-grilled meat on sticks. Now in Ireland we have pizza, doner kebab, tacos, all new additions to our own fast food. Isn't that culturally enriching?

5. My earliest experience of fast food was my fifth birthday when I was brought to MacDonald's with my family as a special birthday treat. The whole thing seemed magical. I sat with a paper birthday crown on my head, and someone brought a birthday cake with candles and got everyone else in the restaurant to sing 'Happy Birthday' to me. I think these fast food places can really make a special time for a family, taking away all the pressure from parents for a special occasion!

6. Fast food is cheaper than other types of food and it is alot healthier than skipping meals. It also stops wasting food because you only order what you can eat. It offers local employment. It is very tasty. It's no surprise really that 56% of students eat fast food weekly! I can just smell those curry chips!

7. The big companies have all introduced health friendly menu options such as salads, fruit cups, yogurt. They have stopped using trans fats to fry in and are now offering grilled and baked options. As far as I can see, fast food will never disappear. There will always be hungry people on the go who need simple food delivered quickly. 'I'm lovin' it!'

> More discussion on the future of fast foods expected. Lively final sentence rounds off the article effectively.

(455 words)

EXAMINER'S COMMENT

GRADE: H2 🔍

P =   13/15
C =   12/15
L =   12/15
M =   4/5

TOTAL = 41/50

- Overall, a solid response addressing the main elements of the task.
- Good use of references to fast food traditions.
- Some focus on the social benefits for young people would have broadened the discussion.
- Expression is functional – apart from some repetition, e.g. 'special' is over-used in paragraph 5.
- Some mechanical flaws ('travelers', 'appartments', 'convienently', 'alot').

1. Write a paragraph as part of a magazine article on a sport or music star you admire. In the article, look at their personality, their achievements and their lasting legacy to the world of sport or music.

Aim for around 120 words.

PROMPT !

- Highlight the star's special talents and achievements.
- Include background details, challenges, important career moments.
- Mention importance and influence as a role model.

CLASS/HOMEWORK ACTIVITY

2. Write a paragraph for inclusion in an article on your school blog, supporting the view that 'Music has no value when you're studying'.

Aim for around 120 words.

PROMPT !

- What evidence do you have that students work better in silence?
- Refer to your own and your friends' experiences.
- Loud background music can reduce concentration.
- Song lyrics can distract students from what they are trying to learn.

Learning aim: To write an effective opinion piece

Opinion pieces are **written articles** that usually appear in the print media or on websites. They express the author's viewpoints and attitudes.

They often focus on people or issues rather than events. An opinion piece offers a **reflective perspective**, informing and entertaining readers.

SOME KEY FEATURES OF OPINION PIECES

● Personal engaging tone

● Lively anecdotes or illustrations

● Aims to get readers thinking critically.

● Conversational and emotive tone

● Language will be reflective and accessible to readers.

Opinion pieces are often structured to include:

● An introduction (e.g. a question, quote or anecdote) engages readers or outlines the central point of the article.

● The main body of the article expands on the theme, sometimes referring to real-life examples.

● A conclusion draws the reflective personal article to a close, perhaps looking towards the future.

SAMPLE OPINION PIECE

The edited extract below is taken from a weekend magazine article featuring young people's experiences of TikTok and other social media platforms.

There is nothing more bizarre and surreal than scrolling through an average TikTok feed. No video is complete without several smaller videos playing at the same time, a veritable hydra of Subway Surfers, Minecraft Parkour and Family Guy.

What is TikTok?

Tiktok is a Chinese social media platform where users share short videos about anything under the sun. The app was launched in 2017 and now has more than a billion users. Its short-clip format has been imitated by Youtube and Instagram.

Positives?

A youth mental health charity, Jigsaw, believes that TikTok gives the opportunity to hand the mic to the teen and say: 'Talk to us. Tell us how it is for you'. The charity commented: 'By God! They'll talk to you on TikTok'.

Negatives?

An adolescent psychotherapist, Dr. Colman Noctor, said, 'Something will gain traction online due to the amount of times it has been viewed, not from the certainty of its information or content. So we follow what is popular rather than what is right'.

What do young people think?

Amina: I'm on TikTok all the time, I go on my phone in the morning and literally sit in bed with my cup of tea on TikTok. It's such a bad habit. I don't think I could actually watch a movie anymore because you have to sit there and only when you're 20 minutes into the movie do you actually realise whether you like it or not.

Izzie: I've Screen Time (a monitoring app) set up on my phone. As in I have x amount of time in a day that I'm allowed to use it ... I don't always follow it, but I try. And it keeps me accountable.

Bel: Like Izzie, I also try to use Screen Time, but for me it kind of never works out. I always end up extending it and giving myself more time.

How can you make your online space more positive?

Ask yourself: Do you feel better or do you feel worse after having been on your phone? Examine who you're letting in and for how long. The app has functionality to both time your usage and block people from your 'For You' page. It's also important to have an open dialogue about the content you're encountering, an open door to a parent or to a guardian.

If you have been affected by any of the issues mentioned above, Jigsaw offers support at jigsaw.ie/chatonline.

WORD POWER

Close analysis of this sample provides an understanding of some of the language skills needed for writing an effective opinion piece.

- Snappy **opening grabs attention** and provides gateway into article, engaging readers.
- **Main body** includes insightful interviews/anecdotes (Amina, Izzie and Bel) and verifiable sources (Dr. Colman Noctor).
- **Questions** used as linking device bring together different aspects of the topic.
- **Conclusion** – reflective closure ('Ask yourself do you feel better') and call to action.

SAMPLE QUESTION (OPINION PIECE)

QUESTION B

Based on your experience of second-level education, write an opinion piece, suitable for publication in a national newspaper (print/online), in which you acknowledge what you see as the strengths of the education you have received, criticise what you see as its weaknesses and make suggestions for its improvement.

NOTE

In responding to this opinion piece question, focus on expressing your views clearly, using language suitable for a national readership. Address all aspects of the question.

SAMPLE ANSWER

1. I am a 17-year-old student from Dublin. I have spent the last 12 years of my life in the Irish education system. My parents cannot afford grinds or private institutes. My best chance to climb the ladder to success is the present Irish education exam system.

> Introduction is personal, clearly focused and succinct.

2. No matter how rich or well-connected you are, when you sit in the exam hall on the day of the Leaving Certificate Examination, you are just another number. It is you, your pen, the exam paper and whatever you have in your brain. I feel that here, at least, I have an equal chance. If I can do well here, no matter my background or connections, I can become more successful. The Leaving Cert is not about your family being rich or poor and this is one of the biggest strengths of Irish education.

3. I also think that the number of subjects we study at Leaving Cert, usually 6 or 7, helps us have a broader view of things. I was talking to my cousin in England, who is sitting his A Levels. They only do three subjects. I was talking about World War 2 and the new Oppenheimer film. He had little idea of his own country's history which I thought was a shame. My granda says you need to know who you are and where you came from.

> Central viewpoint is well developed. The contrast made with the British system is also effective.

4. In contrast to these pluses, the Irish education system has some obvious weaknesses. The large numbers in some classes, sometimes over thirty, prevents even the most dedicated teacher from noticing a quiet pupil who is struggling. I believe that classes should not be bigger than fifteen. This allows teachers to know the students and the students to know each other, a big part of education.

> Solid points about class size and the value of speech training.

5. Another weakness of the education system is that we do not have speech training for all as part of the curriculum. I think this would be great. My parents cannot afford to send me to private drama classes. When I look online at Elon Musk or Tim Cook addressing large numbers of people, I realise that the ability to speak well is an advantage in today's business world. They both may be tech giants, but the ability to communicate matters. I also think it would help students whose first language is not English. Talking tough does not have to be talking rough.

6. I would like to see us keeping the fairness of the Leaving Cert marked by outside examiners, reduce class sizes and introduce speech training for all! I think this would help students to operate on a level playing field. Then it is up to you!

> Summary of main observations rounds off the piece well.

If you have any comments or suggestions on this topic, get in touch: nrogers121@gmail.com.

(455 words)

EXAMINER'S COMMENT

GRADE: H1

P =   15/15
C =   14/15
L =   13/15
M =   5/5

TOTAL = 47/50

- Engaging opening introduces the writer and focuses on the education system.
- Clear personal viewpoints regarding strengths of education, fairness and a range of subjects.
- Well-supported opinions suggesting improvements, e.g. speech training for all students.
- Effective use of linking words: 'In contrast', 'Another'.
- While the expression lacks freshness, it is functional and reflective: 'I think', 'I feel'.
- Conclusion is uplifting and invites a response from readers.

CLASS/HOMEWORK ACTIVITY

Write an opinion piece paragraph for your online school magazine expressing your views on the quality of food options available in school, and suggesting any changes that would improve students' eating habits.

Aim for about 120 words.

PROMPT !

- Does your school provide healthy options for lunch and snacks?
- Should an advertising campaign promoting health foods be introduced?
- Is peer pressure an influence on what you eat in school?
- How could the Science or Home Economics departments help?

Learning aim: To write the text of an engaging podcast

- Podcasts are digital audio programmes or recordings, similar to radio shows.

- They have become increasingly popular over the years, providing a platform for individuals to share their ideas, stories and expertise with a wider audience.

- Different formats include interviews or a commentary by one or more presenters.

- Podcast scripts are written for the ear, not the eye.

- The term 'podcast' comes up from the words 'iPod' and 'broadcast'.

NOTE

While there is **no single format or style** to a podcast, having a pre-prepared script (or outline of what's planned) usually puts everyone at ease – presenter and guests.

FEATURES OF A SUCCESSFUL PODCAST

○ **Good content – an interesting subject or original idea** ○ **Well-organised episodes** ○ **Lively and engaging presenter** ○ **Authentic and relevant guests** ○ **Lots of presenter-to-listener interaction.**

SAMPLE PODCAST

(edited extract: *Physical Activity and Mental Health*)

Voiceover: This podcast is brought to you by the University of Aberdeen.

Bekah: Hello and welcome to our BeWell podcast series. I'm Bekah Walker. Today, we're going to discuss the impact that physical activity can have on our mental well-being. Joining me today, we have Lisa-Marie Schuchardt who is currently studying her Master's in Law. And Kyle Greig from Aberdeen Sports Village.

A huge, warm welcome to you all and thank you so much for joining me. So physical activity, we know, brings a wealth of benefits to our physical health, but also to our mental health too. But what do we mean by being physically active? What does it mean to you? And why should we consider a more active lifestyle?

Kyle: Well, firstly, thank you for having me on the show. I've been running for many years now. Twenty-five years, since I was eight years old. My mum put me in all these different sports clubs and just got me swimming and got me doing martial arts, got me playing football, got me running. And the main one that I kept doing was running.

And I don't know if I was running away from something or somebody. [Laughing] I'm still trying to figure that out. But what I do know is having running and physical activity in my life has made me the person I am today.

Lisa-Marie: I've been also working as a group fitness instructor for the last six years approximately. So, I know that it's really important to move your body. I hate running, I am more of an indoor sports person. So, you see how different it is for everyone. I really love being in the gym. I love group exercises. I love people around me. I love music and I love shutting off my brain.

Bekah: Exercise is something I'm super passionate about. And it's great to just have a conversation with people that feel the same and hopefully help others that maybe are struggling a little bit or thinking for ways, or how do I start to get active? How do I stay active? Why should I be active? And I think and hope from this conversation that we maybe  have helped some people with that. So I would just like to thank you all so much for joining me today and sharing your experiences.

If any of our listeners are looking for ways to get active, we'll share some links to Aberdeen Sports Village in the comments. You can check out the facility. That is where I go most days when I'm exercising. And you can see information about their memberships, too. So thank you again so much to you guys for joining me, our listeners, for tuning in. I hope you enjoyed the episodes. Take care and I'll see you next time.

Edited extract from podcast: Episode 6: Physical Activity and Mental Health, University of Aberdeen.

Close analysis of the language used in the short exemplar above offers a useful guide to key features of an effective podcast.

- The **straightforward intro** engages the existing audience and tells new listeners what the BeWell podcast is about. A series of questions (e.g. 'But what do we mean by being physically active?') gives an overview of why they should listen to this latest podcast.

- Guests are introduced and the presenter's **tone is relaxed**. Both Kyle and Lisa-Marie use anecdotes to share their personal experiences of physical fitness ('I am more of an indoor sports person.'). This gives an authentic feel to the podcast and is likely to appeal to listeners.

- Bekah ensures that the debate does not stray from the central subject. She also emphasises that the podcast is a 'conversation' – an **exchange of views to get listeners thinking**. It's not a lecture.

- The outro **rounds off the discussion** effectively. The presenter thanks guests and audience, and provides some information about local gyms ('we'll share some links to Aberdeen Sports Village in the comments').

SAMPLE QUESTION B (PODCAST)

You have been invited to contribute to a podcast series entitled 'No Pain, No Gain'. The series will explore the importance of keeping fit and exercising in the lives of individuals. Write the text for the podcast in which you: reflect on the importance of fitness and exercising in your own day-to-day life, and discuss some of the benefits and challenges of keeping fit.

SAMPLE ANSWER

1. On a completely personal response, keeping fit isn't a big deal in my daily life. I have played school sports since I was young. But in sixth year, I stopped. Not to study more or anything but to spend more of my free time with friends and playing guitar which is more if an interest for me. I can see what's good about keeping fit and exercising in gyms for some people. But I just don't see it as important right now for me.

> Establishes a point of view and addresses some key elements in the question.

2. I have one friend who is big into gym workouts and constantly exercising. He spends ages doing weights. If I had went with him, I would be fitter I admit but also seriously short of money. What he spends on fancy designer gym gear and especially running trainers at €130 is wild. And he's even charged a euro to get a locker as well. I often think that the exercise programme has taken over his life when he should be out enjoying himself more.

> Anecdotes add interest for listeners. Limited vocabulary and some use of slang.

3. I know there is different viewpoints on exercise and doing PE in school. If I'm been fully honest I think students today are pushed too hard. It's bad enough with regarding points for college. Then we have to balance our study for exams with having a social life. The generation before us weren't under this pressure. There weren't hardly any gyms then and students like my parents didn't feel pressured to keep fit.

> Point needs to be much more developed and clearly expressed.

4. I agree it's a well-known fact that young people who do exercise regularly don't probably get into drugs or other addictions. This is a main benefit. Walking or cycling to school is a cheap way to get exercise and keep fit but what people forget is the weather in Ireland – cold and raining for six months of the year. Which explains why most students get the bus or are dropped off.

> Reasonable discussion on health benefits.

5. I can see the arguements for running and fitness as well. Most people today work in inside office jobs or don't do much actual physical work. Even on building sites it's the machines does the heavy stuff. Good in one way but it means that health issues and challanges could result. The same happens because of fast food. Even though I love takeaway food myself, I also know it's the cause of big problems especially for older people.

6. I suppose I have two different opinions in contrast on this topic. The benefits of exercising are better health and fitness. But exercise can be overdone as well. Like everything else in life, the best idea is moderation. The last thing you want is to burn out and land in hospital.

> Authentic personal tone of voice used to round off the podcast

(440 words)

EXAMINER'S COMMENT

GRADE: H3

P = 11/15
C = 10/15
L = 10/15
M = 4/5

TOTAL = 35/50

- Uneven middle-grade response that touches on some interesting discussion points in response to the question.

- Reasonably focused on personal views, e.g. on gym costs and health benefits of fitness.

- Discussion lacks control at times, e.g. in paragraphs 2 and 3.

- Language use is functional at best and includes some awkward expression (e.g. paragraph).

- Several mechanical errors ('had went with', 'there is', 'been fully', 'arguements', 'challanges').

CLASS/HOMEWORK ACTIVITY

Write a paragraph to be included in a podcast entitled 'Surviving School', in which you express your views on dealing with challenges and maintaining a positive outlook.

Aim for around 120 words.

PROMPT

- Focus directly on the subject (coping with school and staying positive).

- Use relevant anecdotes and illustrations based on personal experience.

- These will be more effective if they're realistic, authentic and brief.

- Your language should aim to help listeners 'visualise' what they hear.

> Podcasting is an amazing way to share your story and inspire others.
>
> **Lewis Howes**

Learning aim: To write effective persuasive speeches

- Comprehending Question B tasks frequently include writing **the text of a short speech**.

- Persuasive speech is a form of public speaking that is usually **more formal** than a talk.

- You may be asked to **argue for or against** a school debate motion, e.g.: 'Reality TV shows are anything but real'.

- **Persuading an audience means getting them to agree** with your point of view.

- The language in a speech will vary depending on the purpose, audience and persona of the writer – all of which will suggest the **appropriate register** or tone.

NOTE

You might be asked to write the text of a speech which is much **more discursive or argumentative than persuasive**. For example: 'Write a thought-provoking speech in which you consider some of the causes and possible solutions to homelessness in Ireland'.

This question is really a talk or opinion piece. While some persuasive language might be appropriate, 'consider' suggests a factual **balanced response** that discusses the subject.

SAMPLE SPEECH

The edited extract below is taken from a speech given by the writer, J. K. Rowling. In the speech, she aims to convince graduating students to see the benefits of failure.

Looking back at the 21-year-old that I was at graduation, is a slightly uncomfortable experience for the 42-year-old that she has become. Half my lifetime ago, I was striking an uneasy balance between the ambition I had for myself, and what those closest to me expected of me.

I wanted to study English Literature. A compromise was reached that in retrospect satisfied nobody, and I went up to study Modern Languages. Hardly had my parents' car rounded the corner at the end of the road than I ditched German and scuttled off down the Classics corridor.

At your age, in spite of a distinct lack of motivation at university, where I had spent far too long in the coffee bar writing stories, and far too little time at lectures, I had a knack for passing examinations, and that, for years, had been the measure of success in my life and that of my peers.

So why do I talk about the benefits of failure? Simply because failure meant a stripping away of the inessential. I stopped pretending to myself that I was anything other than what I was, and began to direct all my energy into finishing the only work that mattered to me. Had I really succeeded at anything else, I might never have found the determination to succeed in the one arena I believed I truly belonged.

I was set free, because my greatest fear had been realised, and I was still alive, and I still had a daughter whom I adored, and I had an old typewriter and a big idea. And so rock bottom became the solid foundation on which I rebuilt my life.

Now, I am not going to stand here and tell you that failure is fun. That period of my life was a dark one, and I had no idea that there was going to be what the press has since represented as a kind of fairy-tale resolution. I had no idea then how far the tunnel extended, and for a long time, any light at the end of it was a hope rather than a reality.

Failure gave me an inner security that I had never attained by passing examinations. Failure taught me things about myself that I could have learned no other way. I discovered that I had a strong will, and more discipline than I had suspected; I also found out that I had friends whose value was truly above the price of rubies.

And tomorrow, I hope that even if you remember not a single word of mine, you remember those of Seneca, another of those old Romans I met when I fled down the Classics corridor, in retreat from career ladders, in search of ancient wisdom: 'As is a tale, so is life: not how long it is, but how good it is, is what matters'.

WORD POWER

Close analysis of this sample provides an understanding of some of the language skills needed for writing an effective speech.

- **Paragraphs 1–2:** Opening **personal tone** and college background details will interest the audience.
- Thought-provoking **rhetorical question** ('So why do I talk about the benefits of failure?') focuses attention on the central theme of the speech.
- Extended **anecdote** about facing personal challenges illustrates and persuasively develops Rowling's argument.
- Use of **repetition** in second-last paragraph ('Failure', 'I') adds emphasis.
- Final **quotation** by the Roman philosopher, Seneca, rounds off the speech on an upbeat, memorable note.

SOME PERSUASIVE WRITING FEATURES

The persuasive features listed below can make your speech more lively and effective – but it's best not to over-use them. These examples are all from a speech opposing zoos.

Persuasive feature	Definition	Example
Anecdote	Real life stories to support your argument.	*Last year I saw a really shocking documentary about a zoo in South America …*
Emotive language	Language that appeals to the audience's feelings.	*Most of us feel a deep sense of shame when we see beautiful animals locked up in cages when they should be free.*
Personal pronouns	Using 'we', 'I', 'you', etc. to make the audience feel included.	*Every single one of us here knows just how bored zoo animals look.*
Rhetorical question	A question which predicts the answer and aimed at gaining support from the audience.	*Wouldn't you feel better if you knew that no animal was being kept in captivity?*
Rule of three	Grouping words or ideas in threes makes them memorable and persuasive.	*Some zoos are cramped, untidy and worst of all, poorly run.*

SAMPLE QUESTION B (SPEECH)

Write the text of a persuasive speech, to be given to your school year group, in which you share your enthusiasm for outdoor pursuits such as hiking, kayaking, etc. In your speech, you should describe your experience of outdoor activities, explain how you became interested in this outdoor pursuit and outline some of the reasons why you would encourage others to take up this hobby.

SAMPLE QUESTION B ANSWER

1. Fellow students. I've been asked to speak about the benefits and advantages of taking part in outdoor activities. Something I totally support and reccomend. From as far back as I remember, my own family were really fond of nature and the whole outdoor life. I have good memories of picnics in the Dublin Mountains and hills overlooking Bray.

> Opening addresses the subject of outdoor pursuits directly. The tone is personal and positive.

2. My parents were serious walker types, so we spent a lot of time just out of the city. The cliffs of Howth was a regular spot. So was Glendalough especially during summer holidays. My experiences of those trips were great ones in which I had a lot of good times. My older brother would make sure that I went with him on the easier walks, so I was never exactly exhausted or anything. We used to ramble off on our own and meet up with the parents later in the evening. Because I was the youngest, my mam always had extra snacks and a treat for me as well.

3. I now understand that being outside together as a family put us all in a good mood. I was encouraged by my parents during my time in secondary to keep doing outdoor activities. So I have got to experience a whole variation of things usually every second weekend. For example, hiking all over County Dublin. And that usually costs almost no money at all. It included a lot of hikes along the coast and once climbing Lugnaquilla which is Wicklow's highest mountain.

> Background family stories take on one key element of the question ('how you became interested').

4. Hill-walking means you get to see fantastic parts of Ireland way off the beaten track. And there are always helpful guides to make sure you won't get lost. Of all the recent outdoor activities I've had, white water rafting gave me the greatest buzz. It's almost impossible to sum up the thrill of a 2-hour trip down the River Liffey.

5. Starting near Dublin centre, you just bounce over fast-flowing water until you get to Strawberry Beds. The actual rafting itself isn't too rigourous. If you're a beginner, you'll be fine. Everything is supervised and kids do this activity all the time. It's just great fun and really boosts your confidence – and you also learn about teamwork.

> Effective illustration of the many benefits ('buzz', 'everything is supervised', 'great fun') is persuasive.

6. Meeting new people is one of the greatest experiences you can have. Over the years, I've met and become life-long friends with others who share my interest in healthy outdoor activities. Being out in nature is also an escape when I feel anxious or down. It's the same probably for thousands of people of our age. We all need a break from the stress of our everyday life.

> Build-up of various other advantages of outdoor activities aims at influencing the audience.

7. How young people spend their free time effects everyone differently. But I can certainly advise the outdoor life. So take yourself out of your comfort zone and broaden your horizon. The great outdoors, as they say, and the simplest things in life are the most enjoyable, and that is what life is about – keeping fit and having fun.

> Although clichéd, the speech is rounded off on an enthusiastic note.

(490 words)

EXAMINER'S COMMENT

GRADE: H2

P = 13/15
C = 12/15
L = 11/15
M = 4/5

TOTAL = 40/50

- Clear sense of purpose and audience, overall.
- Generally addresses the task – but some discussion is more reflective than persuasive (e.g. paragraph 2), which reduces the 'P' mark.
- Good use of illustrative details highlight the benefits of outdoor lifestyle.
- Expression is functional, at times repetitive and awkward (e.g. paragraph 2).
- Some mechanical errors, e.g. 'reccommend', 'ones in which', 'rigourous.', 'effects everyone'.

CLASS/HOMEWORK ACTIVITY

Write the opening paragraph of a persuasive talk, aimed at a group of Transition Year students, outlining some of the arguments in favour of zoos.

Aim for around 120 words.

PROMPT !

- Is seeing different animals up close an enriching experience?
- Do zoos carry out valuable research and conservation programmes?
- Are some rare and endangered species protected?
- Do good zoos have high standards and encourage empathy towards animals?

> Don't raise your voice, improve your argument.
>
> **Desmond Tutu**

20 | Formal Emails

Learning aim: To write an effective formal email

- Emails are among the most commonly used means of communication in the world. While **informal emails are little more than a quick exchange of notes**, most people use them to send documents, music, even pictures and videos.

- A **formal email** is used for business communications, sending enquiries or writing about a job. They serve a clear purpose and get the message across in a professional and polite manner.

- A **job application email** is almost the same as writing a letter – the traditional approach. But it's much faster, of course. Most Irish companies now accept emails from candidates for jobs.

- When you apply for a position via email, you will be up against many other applicants, so **you need your email to be a 'standout' one** to get the reader's attention.

1   Include a professional email address. Your name is best. murphy1900@gmail.com is better than fuzzyonexxx1@yahoo.com. A hiring manager needs to take you seriously.

2   Use an attention-grabbing subject line. Put your name, the role you intend applying for and a reference number (if given). Don't just write 'Job application'. Make it easy for recruiters to link your email with a specific role.

3   Write formally, avoiding 'Hello' or 'Hi'.

4   In the body of the email, outline your knowledge of the role, include a little of what you know about the company and what it does.

5   Write about why you believe you are qualified for the position. Ask to schedule an interview or even a phone call where you can learn more about the job. Indicate possible time-frames.

6   Conclude by thanking the reader for their time. End with 'Best Regards' or 'Sincerely' plus your signature. Do not use 'Cheers'.

7   Include your name, address, email and phone number.

8   Make sure the right attachments, such as your CV, are included.

9   Click 'Send'.

EMAIL EXEMPLAR GUIDE

(Application for a position in tech service company)

- Your name
- Role title
- Job reference number
- Phone number/email address
- Date

JOB APPLICATION EMAIL TEMPLATE

To	
From	
Subject	

To Whom It May Concern (or contact the company for the name of the person conducting the hiring process)

Your need for an [insert job title] as advertised on [location of job listing] is an excellent match to my background and career goals. As a high-impact service delivery professional who is passionate about [insert 1-2 main details from role listing, e.g. creating a genuine connection with each and every customer].

My skills are [explain what skill you have that is part of the requirements for the role].

Highlights of my key skills and experience relevant to your role include: [enter all skills you have relevant to the role and are listed as part of the job requirements, some examples below]

- Excellent verbal and written communication skills
- Ability to build genuine rapport and provide best-in-class service
- Creative thinker with ability to work on own initiative
- Exceptional analytical and problem-solving abilities
- Strong computer literacy and numeracy skills, including Microsoft Office
- Quick learner and can adapt to change with ease.

As a dedicated, loyal and driven individual, I have a positive, can-do attitude and exemplary communication skills. I work well autonomously and as part of a wider group, and can adapt easily to conflicting priorities and critical, deadline-driven workloads.

I always strive to create positive environments and team cultures that harmonise people, processes and systems and drive value-add and commercial benefit.

These abilities can contribute to [enter company name] continued success. I would welcome the opportunity to discuss my background with you in detail and to learn more about your company and goals.

My CV is attached and offers additional information about my specific achievements. I look forward to our conversation.

Sincerely,

(Your name)

Keywords

Most companies use AI to filter applications before they are sent to TA (Talent Acquisition) or HR (Human Resources) teams.

Re-read the job description – add those key words into your application.

If you want someone to see you, show them you have read what they require.

Let's look at the following sample job application emails.

SAMPLE EMAIL 1

To	recruitment@mccanns.com
From	Dantheman@gmail.com
Subject	Job

Hi there,

I want to apply for the job you advertised yesterday online in 'Summer Jobs'.

I think I'd be great for that because I can learn quickly on the job, not a lot of training needed for me!

I know your company, McCann's Builders. My Da buys most of his stuff from you, so I know my way around your yard. Your wood products are very good. I'd like to know when I can come in and have a chat with you about the job and to find the inside track about your company.

Cheers,

Dan

087355666

WORD POWER

Close analysis of this sample provides an understanding of what not to do when writing a formal job application email.

- Unsuitable subject line (no name of applicant, job position or job reference number).
- Unsuitable greeting ('Hi there').
- No reference to specific job advertised ('for the job').
- Incorrect informal tone ('I know your company').
- Inappropriate sign-off ('Cheers').
- Limited vocabulary ('inside track').
- Slight response with no development of points.

SAMPLE EMAIL 2

To	Conlon@silvertechnology.com
From	marylynch1900@gmail.com
Subject	Mary Lynch, Software Developer, Job # 142 337

Dear Mr. Conlon,

I have six years' experience as a Software Developer at Ergon Technology Services. I saw yesterday in Online Business that there was an opening at your firm, Silver Technology. I immediately applied because of your firm's strong reputation for developing new and innovative software.

I am aware that your company rigorously tests a wide variety of software and applications before they are released. As I have experience and expertise in how they were programmed, I can rapidly find glitches, bugs and errors which compromise the security of the software.

I have a Master's degree in Computer Science and have worked exclusively at Ergon Technology Services since graduating. I designed and programmed the engineering software used by students in my college, UCG. I have enjoyed my time at Ergon, but I am looking for the exciting new opportunities offered by Silver Technology.

I have enclosed an up-to-date CV, educational certificates and character references for your consideration. I would love to discuss this role with you further and I look forward to hearing from you soon.

Sincerely,

Mary Lynch
22 Parnell Park
Cork

0879533678

marylynch1900@gmail.com

WORD POWER

Close analysis of this sample provides an understanding of what to do when writing an effective formal email.

- Subject line gives applicant's name, job position and reference number.
- Outlines why she believes she is qualified for the job.
- Gives brief summary of her skill set and experience.
- Asks to schedule an appointment to discuss further.
- Good use of formal language and enthusiastic tone throughout.
- Includes signature, address and contact details at the end.

AVOID!

Make sure you avoid:

- Forgetting any attachments to your email.

- Not changing the template to reflect your personal details.

- Using your current work email address to send new job application email.

- Failing to check what you wrote. Always re-read.

CLASS/HOMEWORK ACTIVITY

Write the opening paragraph/s to be included in an application for a summer job in a local business.

Aim for around 120 words.

PROMPT

- Include subject line (name of applicant, job position, reference number, if given)

- Use an appropriate greeting, tone and language, avoiding slang.

- Detail where and when the job was advertised.

- Explain why you are applying for the job.

- Give a brief summary of your skill set and how you think it will fit the specific job advertised.

Learning aim: To write effective personal journals and reflective diaries

- A journal is a **written record** of your observations, feelings and reflections on your experiences.

- It is also known as a **personal journal**, notebook, diary, log or electronic document.

- Writers, artists and other creative people often keep journals to record important details of their lives and to **explore ideas**.

The personal journal is a very **private document**. A journal (from 'jour', in French, meaning 'day') is a notebook where the author can capture their most intimate and personal thoughts, reflections and feelings. It is written by the author, for the author. The writer records and reflects on life's events, growing in self-knowledge through this thoughtful activity.

- Any style or format can be used.

- Usually organised to track progress or changes.

- True, honest tone, reflecting the writer's feelings and thoughts.

NOTE

Personal journals and diaries are similar. However, a **diary** focuses on daily experiences and events as they happen, whereas a **journal** is usually a more in-depth record of your thoughts and observations on particular topics or issues, etc.

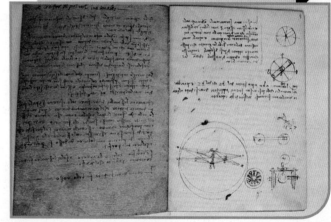

Extract from Leonardo da Vinci's journal

SOME POPULAR TYPES OF JOURNAL

Type of Journal	Details	Purpose
Student/School	Documents and reflects on learning process and outcomes. Good organisational tool.	Helps identify strengths and weaknesses, set goals, monitor progress, improve skills.
Travel	Captures experiences and impressions of visiting different places	Helps to appreciate diversity and beauty of the world, learn about different cultures and histories, recall adventures.
Gratitude	Records the things you are thankful for in your life.	Helps encourage a positive attitude, appreciation of what you have, cope with stress and challenges.
Dream	Describes dreams you have had at night.	Helps explore subconscious mind, understand feelings and desires, unlock creativity.

FIRST IMPRESSIONS

Writer Isabel Hui records her anxiety about her first day of school after moving to a new place. She wanted to make an excellent first impression with what she would wear. It was an unforgettable experience that she would treasure.

When I woke up on August 4, 2016, there was only one thing on my mind: what to wear. A billion thoughts raced through my brain as wooden hangers shuffled back and forth in the cramped hotel closet. I didn't want to come off as a try-hard, but I also didn't want to be seen as a slob. Not only was it my first day of high school, but it was my first day of school in a new state; first impressions are everything, and it was imperative for me to impress the people who I would spend the next four years with. For the first time in my life, I thought about how convenient it would be to wear the horrendous matching plaid skirts that private schools enforce.

It wasn't insecurity driving me to madness; I was actually quite confident for a teenage girl. It was the fact that this was my third time being the new kid. Moving so many times does something to a child's development ... I struggled finding friends that I could trust would be there for me if I picked up and left again. But this time was different because my dad's company ensured that I would start and finish high school in the same place. This meant no instant do-overs when I pick up and leave again. This time mattered, and that made me nervous.

After meticulously raiding my closet, I emerged proudly in a patterned dress from Target. The soft cotton was comfortable, and the ruffle shoulders added a hint of fun. Yes, this outfit was the one. An hour later, I felt just as powerful as I stepped off the bus and headed toward room 1136. But as I turned the corner into my first class, my jaw dropped to the floor.

Sitting at her desk was Mrs. Hutfilz, my English teacher, sporting the exact same dress as I. I kept my head down and tiptoed to my seat, but the first day meant introductions in front of the whole class, and soon enough it was my turn. I made it through my minute speech unscathed, until Mrs. Hutfilz stood up, jokingly adding that she liked my style. Although this was the moment I had been dreading from the moment I walked in, all the anxiety that had accumulated throughout the morning surprisingly melted away; the students who had previously been staring at their phones raised their heads to pay attention as I shared my story.

My smile grew as I giggled with my peers, ending my speech with "and I am very stylish, much like my first period teacher." After class, I stayed behind and talked to Mrs. Hutfilz, sharing my previous apprehension about coming into a new school and state. I was relieved to make a humorous and genuine connection with my first teacher, one that would continue for the remainder of the year.

This incident reminded me that it's only high school; these are the times to have fun, work hard, and make memories, not stress about the trivial details. Looking back four years later, the ten minutes I spent dreading my speech were really not worth it. While my first period of high school may not have gone exactly the way I thought it would, it certainly made the day unforgettable in the best way, and taught me that Mrs. Hutfilz has an awesome sense of style!

Close analysis of this sample provides an understanding of some of the language skills needed for writing an effective journal entry.

- **First-person** pronouns ('I woke up') are obvious features of a personal journal.
- Engaging **reflective tone**: 'I thought how convenient it would be to wear the horrendous matching plaid skirts'.
- Detailed **references are true to life**: 'The soft cotton was comfortable, and the ruffle shoulders added a hint of fun'.
- Focus on **feelings**: 'I was relieved to make a humorous and genuine connection with my first teacher'.
- Authentic, **energetic voice**: 'Mrs. Hutfilz has an awesome sense of style'.

SAMPLE COMPREHENDING QUESTION B

You have been asked to write a reflective personal journal entry about a move you have made from the country to a city. In the piece you should explore the positive and negative aspects of country living, the positive and negative aspects of city life, and give your views on which environment you prefer.

SAMPLE ANSWER

1. Living in the city has its bonuses compared to living in the countryside. If you want to be where things happen, in my opinion, the city is perfect. I just moved to Dublin this year from the countryside because my Dad had been promoted. Goodbye to slow-paced, calm and relaxing, hello to fast-paced, fun and exciting. For me, the city is where it's at.

> Declares which environment is preferred, fulfils part of task. First-person pronouns.

2. In the countryside there is empty. There are very few neighbours, vast areas of land and bogland, stretching as far as the eye can see. Isolated farms, waving crops and grazing animals populate the landscape. So, if you like space and privacy, the country is for you, but not for me.

> Negative aspects of countryside listed, but in general, very little detailed description.

3. I like to conect with people. In Dublin, there are always live music events happening, amazing restaurants and coffee shops that stay open really late. Any day in the city is like being part of a movie. I meet one person which leads to another, leading to new friend groups, a bigger network, and a lot more exiting plans. People to meet, places to go.

> Positive aspects of city recorded, but vague, with few detailed descriptions.

4. I get bored at home easily. I enjoy acting just on impulse and trying new things. Dublin is ticking on my speed. Go into the local library and there you have posters and info about every subject and club in the area. How different from the country where we're lucky to see a local library van.

Positive/negative aspects of country life noted. More detail is given.

5. In the city all it takes is a walk outside to feel very entertained. There are so many great buildings, modern and classic. Parks, people rushing too and fro – it's like a production has been put on just for me. I know you can walk in the countryside and observe nature, but people-watching beats bird-watching any day.

6. Stone-built houses with wooden windows can look good but they can be drafty and chilly. Our new urban house is snug and warm. I am also not sorry to say goodbye to the creepy crawlies. Woodlice and creepy crawly spider friends come with charming weathered open floorboards.

7. Moving home can seem scary and overwhelming. But I believe change is an inevitable part of life. If we accept a positive outlook to change, we won't get burnt out. Change helps us learn, grow and become better people. I am following my dreams, ready for exiting adventures. I'll figure it out as I go along. The world is my oyster!

Conclusion includes some interesting reflection.

(400 words)

Extract from Lewis Carroll's journal

GRADE: H3

P =	11/15
C =	10/15
L =	11/15
M =	4/5

TOTAL = 36/50

EXAMINER'S COMMENT

- Parts of the task are touched on lightly, e.g. positive/negative aspects of country living, which environment preferred.

- No real sense of place. Lack of vivid detailed details impairs credibility of an authentic personal journal.

- No reference to negative aspects of city living reduces the marks for P (purpose).

- Personal engaging tone at times, 'Good bye to …' Hello to …'

- Some humorous touches, 'people-watching beats bird-watching any day'.

- Spelling errors ('isollated', 'conect', 'exiting', 'too and fro', 'drafty') affect the M marks.

CLASS/HOMEWORK ACTIVITY

Write a paragraph for inclusion in your personal journal about your journey to a healthier lifestyle. Explain what led you to choose a healthier lifestyle, some of the challenges you have experienced and the goals you have achieved.

Aim for around 120 words.

PROMPT

!

- Make sure you address all aspects of the question: what led you to choose a healthier lifestyle, the obstacles you faced, the triumphs you experienced and how you hope to continue this process.

- First-person pronouns ('I', 'my', etc.) maintain focus.

- Include detailed descriptions to add credibility.

- Use reflective language: 'I thought', 'I now know', 'I believe'.

> *Journaling is like whispering to one's self, and listening at the same time.*
>
> **Mina Murray**

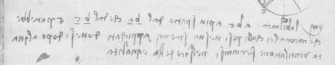

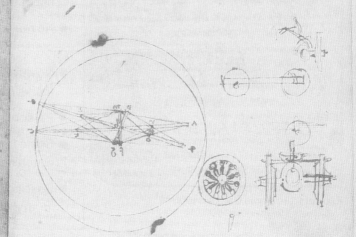

Learning aim: To understand the key elements of an effective blog

BLOG ('WEB-LOG')

- **Blogs are regularly updated websites or web pages which** offer advice and connect people with an online community. They can either be used for personal use or to fulfil an aim.

- Similar to **online diaries**, blogs can focus on a popular lifestyle interests, such as current affairs, music, entertainment, health, education, cooking, sport, travel, fashion, etc.

- Blogs are one of the ways **people can share their advice** on the internet and, of course, influence other people's behaviour.

SOME BLOG POST FEATURES

- Catchy title that pops up easily in search engine
- Addresses readers directly
- Focused on one central idea
- Updated regularly
- Tone: social, chatty, interesting, friendly, provocative, informative
- Short paragraphs, headings and sub-headings
- Underlined phrases emphasise key points
- Links to other pages with similar themes
- Encourages comments or interactions from readers
- Includes blogger's name, contact details and date

NOTE

Successful blogs have **instant appeal** and should be easily scanned. They include links to other web pages, visuals, video clips, etc.

SAMPLE BLOG

The edited blog extract below was posted by Maeve Lee, Noel Baker and Des O'Driscoll.

  BLOG

ELECTRIC PICNIC 2023 REVIEW: TALKING POINTS FROM A FINE WEEKEND IN STRADBALLY

1. WOLFE TONES REVIVAL

The Wolfe Tones' first appearance at Electric Picnic already feels like it has the makings of an annual tradition. Festival organisers say the veteran folk band attracted the biggest crowd ever to the Electric Arena, with thousands joining in the Sunday singalong from outside the huge, packed marquee.

2. THE WEATHER

After the deluge at the 2022 event, and the rather damp summer we've had this year, the good weather in Stradbally through the weekend was particularly appreciated. Festivals are definitely more fun in the sun, don't you agree?

3. NIALL HORAN'S HOMECOMING

Just one hour away from his hometown of Mullingar, former One Directioner Niall Horan was proud as punch to be playing Electric Picnic 2023. Having not played in Ireland in five years, the 'Slow Hands' singer told the crowd on Friday night that he had never been so nervous for a gig. As the audience sang along to every word of his songs, Horan was clearly feeling emotional.

4. BILLIE EILISH OVERCOMES SICKNESS

Another first night highlight was a stellar show from American singer songwriter Billie Eilish who also brought along her brother and co-writer, Finneas. The 'Bad Guy' singer played the festival in 2019 and broke records with the crowd she drew to the main stage.

5. FRED AGAIN DOES IT AGAIN

Saturday night brought British DJ Fred Again's Main Stage debut and festival-goers couldn't have been happier. Last year, the multi-instrumentalist – who has worked with the like of Ed Sheeran and Stormzy – performed on a smaller stage in the festival's Rankin's Woods.

6. AN EMOTIONAL SET FROM THE SCRIPT

The Script were in front of what lead singer Danny O'Donoghue described as the "loudest crowd" they've ever had on Sunday night. The highlight of the performance was a moving tribute to band member Mark Sheehan who passed away in April. 'Earlier on this year we lost our brother,' O'Donoghue said before a huge cheer from the crowd. 'You never realise what you have until it's gone.'

Choking on his words, the lead singer said it was Sheehan who was really looking forward to playing Electric Picnic before dedicating the very emotional 'If You Could See Me Now' to his late friend and band mate as video clips of him played in the background and fans in the crowd wiped away tears.

Festival director, Melvin Benn, flagged that the next event would expand in capacity, going from 70,000 to 75,000. Bigger? Yes. Better? Don't we look forward to finding out?

Post your experiences of Electric Picnic 2023 to irishexaminer.com.

Close analysis of the layout and of language used in the above sample provides a greater understanding of some key features of an effective blog.

- Addresses readers directly – 'don't you agree?', 'Don't we look forward to finding out?'
- Focuses on one central idea – 'Day 1 Highlights' from Electric Picnic 2023.
- Headings and sub-headings aid scanning – 'Niall Horan's home-coming', etc.
- Chatty, informal tone – 'Festivals are definitely more fun in the sun'.
- Encourages comments – 'Post your experiences'.

NOTE

First impressions are important …

- When posting blogs, **titles are what sell the content**. Titles represent content in search engines, email or social media.

- They need to be short, simple, grab attention and **fulfil an aim**. They ask the question readers are asking themselves – and immediately answer it.

- The title *Electric Picnic 2023 Review: Talking Points from a Fine Weekend in Stradbally* **grabs attention**.

SAMPLE QUESTION (BLOG)

QUESTION B

It is the last day of Culture Week in your school and you have been asked to write a blog for your school's website about the events which were held during that week. In your blog, you should describe some of the main events, discuss whether or not Culture Week is regarded positively by students, and speculate about the role you think cultural and arts events will play in schools in future.

SAMPLE ANSWER 1

OUR CULTURE WEEK

1. This week in our school was Culture Week. We had a lot of events going on. There were plays, music and art exhibitions. I liked the art exhibition best because I love art. There were lots of paintings and some sculptures as well. The parents spent time visiting the art exhibition, so that shows it was very popular.

> Makes some attempt to provide an introduction that gives an overview of the week's events.

2. Our teacher Mr Honan is great. He devellops talent by encouraging us all even though some of the students aren't really born artists. But he has a very good way of helping you find out what you're best at doing, whether it's sketching or doing life portraits.

3. There were other events in the library to do with book workshops and litriture. Every English class wrote book reviews and these were on display. The computer room was also involved with letting students do creative art designs and using a robot to make a new piece of art. Other classes were told how to use their computers to make up funky music.

> Lists a number of the main arts events and responds personally to some of them.

4. There were also one or two good plays. Some of the sixth years put on extracts from their Leaving Cert play. It was King Lear, but in modern dress. They didn't have an old king arguing about dividing up his land. It was a modern parent and his children arguing about pocket money. The three daughters had to say they loved him to recieve the most money. Everyone thought it was cringy. But the ones studying the play thought it was good.

5. These were the best events in my opinion. You can write your own comment below if you agree or disagree with me. I think Culture Week should be on every year, especially the Art Exhibition. Not everyone plays sports. It's a good thing that culture week didn't ignore the students who like art and music. If your paintings are put on show in the assembly hall everybody that had went there know you have a talent even though it's not given the same hype as sport. So that's a good reason for having a culture week in future years.

> Interesting viewpoint about the value of school cultural events rounds off the blog.

6. I think it is great for students to hear parents say that they liked their pictures and sketches. It's good for everyone and gives the students a good boost.

That's all for now.

Comments to stcillians.ie

(385 words)

GRADE: H4

P =   11/15
C =   10/15
L =   9/15
M =   4/5

TOTAL = 34/50

EXAMINER'S COMMENT

- Mid-grade answer focused reasonably well on culture week but went off point at times (e.g. in paragraph 2).

- Blog lacks a catchy title. There were no sub-headings, date or blogger's name.

- One of the tasks in the question ('whether or not Culture Week is regarded positively by students') was reasonably well addressed.

- Very little discussion about 'the role you think Culture Week will play in schools in future'.

- Note-like expression, limited vocabulary and very little development of points.

- Some mechanical errors ('devellops', 'litriture', 'recieve', 'had went').

SAMPLE ANSWER 2

CULTURE WEEK CALL OUT

Jennifer Murphy

Culture Week in our school, St. Cillian's, Newbridge, took place on 11th-15th October with a brilliant selection of drama, poetry, music and art.

HIGHLIGHTS

Day 1

A stunning art exhibition took place in the school hall. There were 50 paintings and 20 sculptures. The standard was amazing! You all saw it! The students whose work was on display were present to answer any questions or comments from parents and visitors. At the back of the Hall a music quartet played some classical music and tea and refreshments were served by the Home Economic Department!

> Lively informative intro. Catchy title and sub-head encourage readers to continue. Details provide a vivid sense of atmosphere.

Don't you agree that it's lovely to hear positive feedback on work on which you spent so much time? The buzz was electric!

Day 2

A modern take on the Leaving Cert Shakespearean play, *King Lear*, took place in the Assembly Hall. It was just for senior students. They sat in a semi-circle while a parent had his children negotiate how much pocket-money they were going to get depending on how much they said they loved him. One child said nothing and got nothing. They had to do this in front of three of their friends. The student discussion afterwards was quite intense. 'Gross!' 'Unfair!' were some of the comments. 'Embarrassing!' 'I can't believe it!' echoed around the Assembly Hall. The students all agreed it was a good way to introduce the message of abuse of power to them.

> Effective description again re-creates a dramatic scene and an authentic sense of the student voices.

PLUS OR MINUS?

Students were really upbeat about their Culture Week experiences. Many I spoke to said it made them see some students in a different – and creative – light. Others said it made them proud to belong to a school which could put on so many arts events. They enjoyed seeing the parents view their work and make positive comments about it. Overall, it was a big plus! Apart from the obvious development of creativity and self-expression, the arts increase young people's confidence and can really motivate them – which in turn improves well-being and (dare I say it?) school attendance.

> Perceptive overview comments, clearly and succinctly expressed, using fresh language.

ROLL ON NEXT YEAR!

I'm sure you will agree that Culture Week has a bright future. Many of the First and Second Years who were only onlookers were already excitedly discussing what they would put on for 'their' Culture week. Would they produce a drama of their own or exhibit a picture or play in a group? As for me, I think it was a great experience for all and brought the school closer together as a community.

Comment to stcillians.ie

Ends on a positive note that is likely to encourage readers to support future arts events.

(415 words)

EXAMINER'S COMMENT

GRADE: H1

P =	15/15
C =	15/15
L =	15/15
M =	5/5

TOTAL = 50/50

- Effective top-grade answer used an appealing title, name, date and sub-headings.
- Detailed and developed focus on all key aspects of the question.
- Interesting and thought-provoking points throughout.
- Expression was varied and well controlled.
- Tone was personal, chatty and enthusiastic.
- Very good sense of updating posts and of student audience.

CLASS/HOMEWORK ACTIVITY

Write a paragraph to be included in a blog for your school website on Sports Week in your school.

Aim for around 120 words.

PROMPT!

- Describe some of the main sports events.
- Discuss the extent to which Sports Week is regarded positively by students.
- Give your own views on the atmosphere in the school during the week.
- Explore the role you think Sports Week will play in your school in future years.

Successful blogging is not about one-time hits. It's about building a loyal following over time.

Sahil Sain

Learning aim: To understand key elements of effective introductions

- An **introduction presents something new** to an audience, e.g. the opening section of a programme for a film festival or art exhibition.

- Introductions to books (whether fiction or non-fiction) also **spark people's curiosity** and stimulate interest.

- Book introductions can be **written by the author or by someone else**, such as an editor or celebrity.

- In the Leaving Cert English exam, you may be asked to write a Comprehending B introduction, e.g. to a new collection of Irish fiction. A good introduction will always **engage readers**, drawing them in with an emotional connection, and convincing them that the book is worth reading.

WRITING EFFECTIVE INTRODUCTIONS

- Outline **your own background** and explain (very briefly) how you got involved in the project. But don't make the introduction about you.

- Why should people read this book? That is the key question. **You're promoting the book** and introducing readers to buy something you hope will interest them.

- Mention some of the things that appealed to you and use **specific examples** from the book whenever possible.

- Help **readers trust what you have to say** by keeping your writing tone personal, relaxed and conversational.

> **NOTE**
>
> **Front matter** is information about a book which comes before the main text.
>
> An **introduction** prepares readers for what to expect and focuses on the book's content (subject matter).
>
> A **foreword** differs from an introduction in that it is written by someone other than the author and tells readers why they should read the book.
>
> A **preface** is a short piece explaining the author's own experience of writing the book.

SAMPLE INTRODUCTION

Welcome to *Interesting Stories for Curious Kids,* a fascinating collection of the most interesting, unbelievable and craziest stories on earth! This book will introduce you to some of the strangest facts on our incredible planet but in a way that is fun for you!

You'll definitely learn an enormous amount reading this book, but I guarantee you'll never be bored. Since you have a busy life with family, friends, school, and hobbies, the way you read this book is entirely up to you. You can read it from cover to cover like a traditional book, or you can skip around and not miss a thing.

Each of the stories is also fairly short, so you don't have to spend a lot of time reading them. The stories in this book come from different categories of human life, but the important thing is they are written to appeal to kids your age. That's right; this book was written with the interests of kids your age in mind!

Some of the research was even done by kids your age! So when you read about these historical stories, it will also be something you'll find fun. For instance, you'll read about some of the most powerful kids in history, from ancient Egyptian pharaohs to Chinese and Japanese emperors. You'll also learn about how the Vikings invented sledding, skiing, and skating.

And what about school? Well, you'll learn how schools a long time ago were different, and sometimes the same, as they are today. Plus, for all you science fans, don't worry, we've got you covered! There are plenty of fun science stories in here that answer some questions you and your friends have no doubt discussed.

What's the smartest animal in the world? How many bones are in the human body? How are llamas related to camels? How do parrots talk? Even if science isn't your best subject, you're sure to find something you like and information that you didn't know. There are also a few fun science experiments that you can do to impress your friends and family. We show you how it's impossible to crush an egg in the palm of your hand and how to mummify a hot dog – yes; you read that last part correctly!

Dive in and read about some of your favourite movies, books, and entertainers to learn how they got their starts. You may be surprised that some of your favourite movies were remakes of movies that your parents – and even your grandparents – once thought were cool.

Finally, kids all over the world like a good scary story from time to time, so we have a few here you are certain to like, plus a few stories that defy categorisation. So sit back, relax, and open the pages of this book to travel into another world where learning is fun.

Once you read a few of the stories in this book, you're sure to impress your friends and maybe even win a few arguments. But more than anything – just remember to have fun!

Close analysis of the language used in the above exemplar offers a useful guide to writing an effective introduction.

- Opening paragraphs are informative and straightforward, **addressing young readers directly**. The language is simple and the relaxed tone invites 'kids' to enjoy the new collection: 'you'll never be bored'.

- Details about what the foreign settings and **exciting 'worlds'** of these stories (e.g. 'Japanese emperors') are likely to interest young readers.

- The **focus on education** ('plenty of fun science stories') will also appeal to parents and guardians.

- Ending is upbeat with the **emphasis on enjoying learning** ('travel into another world where learning is fun').

THE HORROR GENRE

Before horror movies, people relied on books to scare themselves. And many of the strange creatures that are now featured on the big screen – including vampires, werewolves, zombies and ghosts – can trace their origin back to medieval times.

SAMPLE QUESTION (BOOK INTRODUCTION)

QUESTION B

Write the introduction for *All Kinds of Scary*, a new collection of horror stories. In your introduction you should: describe how you became interested in horror fiction and films, discuss some of the main qualities that are essential in a good horror story, and explain why you recommend this particular collection of stories to readers.

PLANNING YOUR RESPONSE

- For a successful response, planning is essential. **Study the wording of the question closely** to understand all elements of the task.

- Your introduction should **encourage readers** to engage with the new collection of horror fiction. The writing should be aimed at fans of horror stories as well as readers in general.

WHAT TYPE OF LANGUAGE WILL I USE?

- Personal, informative, persuasive, etc.

HOW DO I STRUCTURE (ORGANISE) MY RESPONSE?

- **Brief introduction**, naming the title and outlining the horror genre.

- **Address three main elements of the task** (though not necessarily equally).

- These include: your **own interest** in horror, **qualities** of a good horror story, why you **recommend** this new collection.

SAMPLE ANSWER

1. I have been asked to write the introduction for this new collection of horror stories, *All Kinds of Scary*, which is just the kind of book I myself love to read. As a young adult who has always liked horror, I really enjoyed these new short stories.

2. I've seen great horror movies over recent years – like *The Shining* and *Contagion*. I'm also a fan of Stephen King's brilliant books. *Misery* and *Carrie* are just two of my all-time favourites. The film that first got me interested in horror was the *Blair Witch Project*. Three teenagers go hiking and try to make a documentary film about a witch in the wood. They get lost and everything soon goes wrong, so they get more and more scared. They're not the only ones.

> Personal approach, using a relaxed conversational tone to address the first part of the task.

3. Most of the movie takes place during daylight which was the first surprise. But it showed that horror stories don't have to always be in the dark. There are no monsters or gross violence or blood-curdeling scenes, but there is something much scarier. You don't actually see any horror, but it's all hinted at. One of the characters goes missing, and then a small bag of teeth are found outside their tent. Basically your imagination takes over and the fear really grows.

4. This is the most important quality of a good horror story. In my opinion the best ones are not the obvious slasher bloodbaths. Some terrifying stories deal with graveyards and ghosts. These supernatural aspects are in the novel *Carrie*, for example. The main character has special powers to move objects by using just her mind. She uses this trick to take terrible revenge on her classmates.

> Good use of examples of the horror genre and the way fear is based on suggestion.

5. Shock is another feature of horror. The unexpected can be totally scary. Many stories drop clues about what awful things could happen later on. This makes readers uneasy and totally stressed out because they know someone or something terrible may appear at any moment.

6. The more relatable a horror story is, the scarier. In the novel *Cujo*, Stephen King took an ordinary St. Bernard dog and turned it into a total monster. There are some very grusome scenes at the end, but all the suspense comes from imagining what might happen.

> Short paragraph makes a strong point about foreshadowing.

7. In writing this introduction, I can safely say that horror fans will really be on the edge of their seats with these new stories – just like I was. Even the title had me hooked. There is something for everyone, such as zombies and vampires breaking into homes while totally innocent people are asleep. If you love the thrill of being absolutely terrified by a creepy story, this new collection of ten seperate stories will really get your imagination going. So prepare to be scared.

> More expected on the new book's highlights. However, the lively, enthusiastic ending encourages readers.

(450 words)

EXAMINER'S COMMENT

GRADE: H2

P = 13/15
C = 12/15
L = 11/15
M = 4/5

TOTAL = 40/50

- Solid response which tackles the main elements of the task well.
- Some insightful ideas about the qualities and features of the horror genre.
- More focus on the new book's contents – e.g. making up titles for one or two stories – would have been effective.
- Uses an appropriate tone to promote both the horror genre and the new collection.
- Expression is functional and most discussion points are clearly stated.
- Some mechanical errors ('blood-curdeling', 'are found', 'grusome', 'seperate').

CLASS/HOMEWORK ACTIVITY

Write the introductory paragraph for a new science fiction novel, entitled *The Last Alien Invasion*.

Aim for around 120 words.

PROMPT !

- Briefly introduce yourself and outline the sci-fi genre.
- What does the title word 'Last' suggest?
- When is the story set? Who is the central character?
- What makes this novel different to others about extra-terrestrials?
- Does the introduction intrigue readers? But without giving away too much information?

- **Open letters are published publicly** – usually in emails to newspapers or online. Sometimes they are read out on radio or television.

- While an open letter can be addressed directly to specific person, a group or an organisation, they are all **intended to be read by a wide audience**.

- **Critical open letters often protest about something**. These are generally addressed to well-known politicians, or other public figures are especially common.

- The writing **style can be either formal or informal**. Some open letters raise serious issues of public interest, e.g. about the country's health service. These are generally informative and persuasive.

WHY PEOPLE WRITE OPEN LETTERS

- To express strong views on a particular issue.
- To encourage further debate.
- To ask for public support.
- To look for attention.

NOTE

A personal open letter is very **like a blog**. The tone can be humorous or sarcastic, especially if it is an open letter of complaint.

SAMPLE OPEN LETTER

The edited letter extract below was written by professional footballer, Marcus Rashford. He sent it to British MPs in 2020 asking them to reconsider their decision to end free school dinner vouchers.

1. My story to get here is all-too-familiar for families in England: my mum worked full-time, earning minimum wage to make sure we always had a good evening meal on the table. But it was not enough. The system was not built for families like mine to succeed, regardless of how hard my mum worked.

2. As a family, we relied on breakfast clubs, free school meals, and the kind actions of neighbours and coaches. Food banks and soup kitchens were not alien to us; I recall very clearly our visits to Northern Moor to collect our Christmas dinners every year. It's only now that I really understand the enormous sacrifice my mum made in sending me away to live in digs aged 11, a decision no mother would ever make lightly.

3. This is not about politics; this is about humanity. Looking at ourselves in the mirror and feeling like we did everything we could to protect those who can't, for whatever reason or circumstance, protect themselves. Political affiliations aside, can we not all agree that no child should be going to bed hungry? In England today, 45% of children in Black and minority ethnic groups are now in poverty.

4. Parents like mine would rely on kids' clubs over the summer break, providing a safe space and at least one meal, whilst they work. Today, parents do not have this as an option. If faced with unemployment, parents like mine would have been down at the job centre first thing Monday morning to find any work that enables them to support their families. Today, there are no jobs.

5. As a Black man from a low-income family in Wythenshawe, Manchester, I could have been just another statistic. Instead, due to the selfless actions of my mum, my family, my neighbours, and my coaches, the only stats I'm associated with are goals, appearances and caps. I would be doing myself, my family and my community an injustice if I didn't stand here today with my voice and my platform and ask you for help.

6. The Government has taken a 'whatever it takes' approach to the economy – I'm asking you today to extend that same thinking to protecting all vulnerable children across England. I encourage you to hear their pleas and find your humanity. Please reconsider your decision to cancel the food voucher scheme over the summer holiday period and guarantee the extension.

7. This is England in 2020, and this is an issue that needs urgent assistance. Please, while the eyes of the nation are on you, make the U-turn and make protecting the lives of some of our most vulnerable a top priority.

Source: www.independent.co.uk, Melissa Reddy, Senior Football Correspondent, Sunday 14 June 2020

Close analysis of this sample provides an understanding of some of the language skills needed for writing effective open letters.

- **Paragraphs 1–2:** Opening tone **personal tone** and family background details targets readers' sympathy.

- **Paragraph 3:** Focuses on the **central issue about the need for free school dinner vouchers:** 'no child should be going to bed hungry'. Use of statistics adds support to the argument.

- **Paragraphs 4–5:** The **writing throughout is clear** and straightforward, easily understood by a wide audience ('Today, there are no jobs').

- **Paragraphs 6–7:** The ending calls upon the government to help combat child food poverty. The tone **is polite and persuasive**, emotional without being sentimental: 'Please reconsider your decision to cancel the food voucher scheme'.

CLASS/HOMEWORK ACTIVITY

Many students feel strongly about particular issues, such as freedom of speech. Write the opening paragraph of an open letter, to be published on a popular social media platform, stating your views on this topic.

Aim for around 120 words.

SAMPLE ANSWER 1

I totally believe in freedom of speech and have no time for any sort of censorship. That's why I'm writing this open letter. If we're not allowed to say what we're thinking, it would be like living under a dictator. Take crime. If a suspect can't tell his side of the story in the court, he'll end up in prison. Young teenagers are often accused in the wrong. So they have to be able to give their side of what happened. Not being allowed to speak out would lead to a dictator state. Without basic freedom. I'm a total believer in human rights and freedom of speech is a basic right. End of story.

EXAMINER'S COMMENT

- Strong opening focusing on one general point.
- Very little sense of introducing other issues related to freedom of speech.
- Expression is note-like and repetitive.
- Reasonably clear, overall. Solid mid-grade standard.

SAMPLE ANSWER

Freedom of speech is high on the wish list for young people. Students have every right to be listened to and their views respected. In the old days, we were seen and not heard. However, one thing I've learned is that there has to be some limits on free speech. Everyone believes that free expression is a basic right. But does that mean we should be able to say absolutely anything we want all the time? There has to be rules about things such as hate speech, racial abuse or sexist comments. The same goes for cyber bullying and obscene language, especially towards children. Free speech is a complicated subject and a balanced approach is needed in doing what's appropriate. But who decides what's a fair balance?

EXAMINER'S COMMENT

- Confident top-grade introductory paragraph focuses on free speech throughout.

- Insightful overview of some key points concerning this 'complicated subject'.

- Expression is clear and the use of questions invites a response from readers.

- Final sentence raises an interesting follow-up issue for discussion.

CLASS/HOMEWORK ACTIVITY

Write a paragraph for inclusion in an article on your school website in which you discuss the value and importance you place on always telling the truth.

Aim for around 120 words.

PROMPT

!

- Does honesty ensure self-respect?

- Can friends and others always rely on you?

- Is life simpler for the honest person? No fears of lies being discovered?

- Any dangers of being rude or offending others?

COMPREHENDING QUESTION B HOMEWORK ASSIGNMENTS

 Allow about 40 minutes and aim for around 450 words.

1. QUESTION B (50 MARKS)

Imagine that you are a young adult refugee who has recently been granted asylum in Ireland. Write the text of a **talk** you would deliver to a group of Sixth Year students, explaining why you chose this country and your first impressions of Ireland, and discussing some of the positive and negative aspects of Irish life that you have observed.

PROMPT !

- Take time to **plan** your response to include the four elements of the task (why you chose Ireland, first impressions, some positive and negative aspects).

- Think about a suitable **register and tone**. Will your talk be personal? Informative? Descriptive? Reflective? Persuasive? Or a mix of these?

- Aim for a clear sense of **engagement with the student audience**, using appropriate language.

2. QUESTION B (50 MARKS)

Write an **email** job application for a summer job in a local business. Refer to the specific job advertised and explain why your skill set and experience will be a good fit for the position advertised. Detail what you know about the local business and its products and/or services. Ask for an opportunity to discuss your background and to learn more about the business.

PROMPT !

- Include **subject line details and** use an appropriate formal greeting, tone and language.

- Briefly **explain why** you are applying for this particular job.

- Outline **your skill set** and how you think it will suit the specific job advertised .

3. QUESTION B (50 MARKS)

You have been asked to contribute an **opinion piece** for a popular social media platform about the increasing focus on wellbeing in Ireland's secondary schools. In your article you should: describe some of the positive effects of wellbeing evident in schools today, discuss whether or not, in your view, the focus on wellbeing can sometimes be a negative influence, and suggest some ideas for promoting wellbeing in schools in the future.

PROMPT !

- Address the **three main elements** in the task (although not necessarily equally).
- Think about a suitable **register and tone**. Will the writing be personal? Informative? Critical? Or a mix of these?
- Aim for a clear sense of **engagement with a general audience**, using appropriate language.

4. QUESTION B (50 MARKS)

You have decided to write an online **review** of a popular novel aimed at young adults. In your review, outline the book's the genre and plot. Comment on the positive and negative aspects of the book to support your opinion about whether or not it will appeal to teenage readers.

PROMPT !

- Address the **elements** in the task (genre, plot, positive/negative aspects and the novel's appeal).
- Think about a suitable **register and tone**. Will the writing be objective? Informative? Critical? Or a mix of these?
- Aim for a clear sense of **engagement with the young adult audience**, using appropriate language.

COMPOSING OVERVIEW

Composing is the most important question on the Leaving Cert English paper and is worth **100 marks** (25% of the overall total). The question offers students an opportunity to display a variety of writing skills and a flair for language use.

Aim for 850–900 words (written over 80 minutes).

POPULAR COMPOSITIONS INCLUDE:

- Personal essays
- Short stories
- Descriptive essays
- Online/magazine articles
- Discursive essays
- Persuasive speeches
- Informative talks/opinion pieces

Composing questions will usually be associated with **a particular language genre**. The prescribed genres (types) of language use will be included among the composition titles:

- Informative
- Argumentative
- Persuasive
- Narrative
- Aesthetic

> **NOTE**
>
> 'It is accepted that to classify language in this way is artificial. The general functions of language outlined here will continually mix and mingle, within texts and genres. So, there can be an aesthetic argument, persuasive narrative or an informative play.' (Department of Education English Syllabus)

COMPOSING QUESTION SEC MARKING SCHEME

Marks are awarded by reference to the **PCLM** criteria for assessment:

CLARITY OF PURPOSE (30%)

This refers to engagement with the task. Has the candidate engaged with the question? Relevance, focus, originality, freshness, clear aim and understanding of genre are rewarded here.

COHERENCE OF DELIVERY (30%)

This refers to the ability to sustain the response over the entire answer. Continuity of argument, sequencing, management of ideas, use of examples, control of register and creative modelling are all rewarded in this section.

EFFICIENCY OF LANGUAGE USE (30%)

This refers to control of language to achieve clear communication. Has the candidate used language suitable for the task? Vocabulary, syntax, paragraphing, punctuation and use of lively expression are examined here.

ACCURACY OF MECHANICS (10%)

This refers to accuracy of spelling and grammar.

LEAVING CERT ESSAYS – PURPOSE AND STYLE

Personal Essay

Purpose: To share and reflect on personal experiences

Style: Take a personal view, use of personal pronouns 'I', 'me', etc. anecdotes, reflective observations, insights, confessional tone, humour

Speech/Talk

Purpose: To convince an audience to agree with your point of view

Style: Language of persuasion and/or argument, awareness of audience, use of references, rhetorical questions, emotive impact, exaggeration, personal anecdotes

Short Story

Purpose: To write a narrative of imagined events and characters

Style: Use of plot, characterisation, setting, conflict, tension, atmosphere, dialogue, narrative shape, tension, flashback, climax, suggestion, aesthetic qualities

Feature Article

Purpose: To discuss, inform, entertain and persuade readers

Style: Opinion piece – online or in the print media – discussing current affairs or issues of interest using engaging language, detailed description, personal anecdotes, exaggeration, humour

Descriptive Essay

Purpose: To describe a person, place or thing in vivid detail

Style: Detailed descriptive writing, imagery, setting, anecdote, atmosphere, appeal to senses, fresh vocabulary, engaging aesthetic features

Discursive/Argumentative Essay

Purpose: To explore various aspects of a specific topic, issue or controversy

Style: Investigative approach, objective supportive evidence, reflective arguments and counter-arguments, analysis, evaluation

Aesthetic Writing

Purpose: To use language imaginatively, showing its subtlety and beauty

Style: Features include sensuous imagery, evocative tones, lyrical qualities and poetic, figurative language, e.g. metaphors, similes, personification, etc.

Informative Writing

Purpose: To offer a factual account and to educate in an interesting way

Style: Explanation using informative language, presenting factual evidence, balanced analysis, data, statistics, challenging misinformation

---

NOTE

- Always aim to **find your own voice** when writing essays or short stories.
- Textbook **exemplars** of sample essays and stories illustrate a variety of responses and different standards of answering.
- They **should not be recycled** in the examination.

Personal Essays

Learning aim: Analysing reflective personal writing

A **personal essay** explores your thoughts and feelings about a subject or issue in an engaging and interesting way. It should be both **personal** and **reflective**.

WHAT IS PERSONAL WRITING?

You are **sharing your experiences** and expressing your views – for example, 'I was really proud of my TY class who raised €500 for the charity 'Soup Kitchens in Ireland'.

WHAT IS REFLECTIVE WRITING?

Reflective writing means thinking deeply about past experiences, people and events. **How were you affected?** What lessons did you learn? How will it affect your behaviour in future?

For example: 'In my last school, I was bullied for a few weeks. It was horrible! I realised I had a choice. I could allow it to happen or I could stand up for myself. It was up to me to choose!'

> **NOTE**
>
> Reflective essays involve more than just describing what happened. There needs to be a sense of development based on what you have learned. Phrases such as, 'At the time', 'Thinking back' and 'I now understand' can start the reflective process.

EFFECTIVE PERSONAL WRITING

- Decide on **what** you want to explain, share or understand
- Identify your **target audience**
- Use **descriptive, discursive** language
- Include **anecdotes** (real or fictional personal stories)
- Write in an **honest tone**, using first person pronouns: 'I', 'me', etc.
- Include **reflective insights** (considering what the experience you have described meant to you)

SAMPLE PERSONAL WRITING QUESTION

Identify two features of reflective personal writing in the following extract and comment briefly on the effectiveness of each.

Aim for around 120 words.

MY CULTURAL LIFE

The writer Emma Dabiri shares the music that has shaped her life and work.

Bob Marley's *Survival* was such a foundational album when I was growing up. When I was little, my parents took me to a signing he did. The album cover is all of the flags of the newly independent African countries and on the poster he wrote: 'To Emma One Love Jah Guide. Bob Marley'. The righteous sense of justice that informs Rastafarianism had a profound effect on me. Musically, I'm having a real Irish-trad moment right now! I'm listening to a band called The Dubliners, whose heyday was the 1960s, as well as other Irish folk bands.

SAMPLE ANSWER 1

This extract by the writer Emma Dabiri is definitely an example of features of reflective personal writing in which she share the music that shaped her life and work. It's mostly about getting a poster signed. It had the flags of the newly independent African countries printed on it. Emma also talks about an Irish band she heard about called The Dubliners. This shows her personal love for music and that it has changed from when she was little. Her top bands of all time at the moment are Irish folk. Emma is very honest in sharing her music likes and dislikes in a personal way.

EXAMINER'S COMMENT

- Relies largely on summarising – with almost no discussion about the reflective style.

- Some of the points are copied directly from the paragraph.

- More focus on tackling the two parts of the question would have improved this basic answer.

SAMPLE ANSWER 2

This piece of writing is both personal and reflective. The writer uses a personal anecdote about meeting Bob Marley when she was a child. He made a big impact on her and introduced her to his music and ideas about justice and freedom for African countries. She was very influenced by his 'foundational album' when growing up'. When she remembers this time, she knows that it had a 'profound effect' on her. Emma Dabiri's personality comes through in this short piece of writing. The fact that meeting Bob Marley changed her life is evidence that she is a very passionate character.

- Focuses on the two aspects of the question (finding examples of reflective personal features and discussing their effectiveness).
- Clear understanding of Dabiri's reflection ('foundational album', 'profound effect').
- Engages closely with the extract and develops points about the style.
- Good controlled expression throughout this top-grade response.

SAMPLE PERSONAL ESSAY

Write a personal essay in which you reflect on some of the things that make you 'glow' with excitement and happiness.

MARKING SCHEME GUIDELINES

- **P:** Focus – a **personal essay,** in which you reflect on some of the things which you 'glow' with excitement and happiness.
- Understanding of **genre** – the effective use of some elements of personal writing, e.g. written in the first person, reflective tone, use of authentic personal voice, personal anecdotes.
- Observations, revealing personal insights, etc.

SAMPLE PERSONAL ESSAY ANSWER

1. I have a beautiful view which makes me 'glow' with excitement and happiness. I look at it every day from my bedroom window. I'm not boasting about my dad's gardening or that I live in some rich mansion with huge landscaped gardens or anything. Because my view is totally free and it's all mine.

2. On a summer's morning I open my pale blue curtains and gaze dreamily from my bed at the blue sky beyond. I can make out the storm clouds sometimes, or on brighter days, the breaks in the white mist as the sunlight tries to break through. I sit up and stretch. The ordinary familiar view of the grass and the well cared for hedge. Then the washing line and the grey and white wall around the vegetable patch come into view. This is my view and I just love it. The white, grey, and blue say to me it's time to face another brand new day. I wish I was always totally full of energy at the thought of another new day, but when I gaze at my view, I want to just curl up and go back to sleep.

> Some good detailed development of this special place. Over-emphasis on colours.

3. But the night and the darkness pass. This little ordinary view seems to be quietly whispering. The hedge at the bottom of the garden, green in summer and brown from the sea-winds in winter, sighs softly. It protects me from the field beyond with its great staring cows and noisy chugging tractor. Like a soft embrace, it protects me from the ugliness of the world.

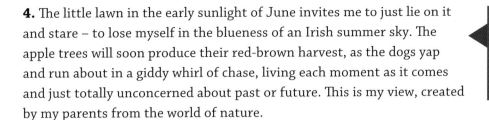

4. The little lawn in the early sunlight of June invites me to just lie on it and stare – to lose myself in the blueness of an Irish summer sky. The apple trees will soon produce their red-brown harvest, as the dogs yap and run about in a giddy whirl of chase, living each moment as it comes and just totally unconcerned about past or future. This is my view, created by my parents from the world of nature.

> Expression lacks control and is repetitive – 'just' and 'totally' over-used.

5. Yet I can't help feeling that this is their view, it is their dream, what they always wanted to look at. But is it enough for young people? My sisters have left home, flown the proverbiel nest. They rarely get to see what I see, the view my parents created for us. Soon, I too, must leave this nest. I will have to deal with the world beyond my hedge, I must give up the identity given to me by my parents at birth, and create who I myself must become. I have looked, but I cannot imagine that person in the garden. Is she to be found in the distant walls of a faraway university or in the tall buildings of the modern city?

6. I look out again on my view. The white fluffy clouds move across the vast blue sky. Will I travel across that huge area of blue? I don't want to be hemmed in like the cows and small apple trees. I think if I stay here, I too will just stare as an idle person or become bitter like the apples. I think travel and new experiances broaden a person. I don't want to be like the old pond at the back of the vegetable patch, going nowhere, just becoming slowly decayed.

> Personal reflection – but losing sight of the 'excitement and happiness' elements of the question.

7. My parents think this is the perfect place to be. So they just can't understand me wanting to leave home. 'Look what we have here, a paradise,' Mum says. 'I have worked day and night to create this perfect place for us,' Dad moans. But they had their fun many years ago, travelling all over the world. Even going absieling down a huge waterfall. Lounging for days on sandy beaches, tasting beautiful food. 'But the world has changed,' they complain. 'It's not safe anymore!' But I need to find that out for myself. I don't want to hide away totally, scared of living. It's my life, not theirs – and I have to follow my own heart. I must go, I cannot stay.

8. My view is so beautiful, but my future is not here. I just can't ignore the world any longer. I just must join in. My beautiful view will remain in my memory. I will revisit my old home, as the famous Irish poet William B Yeats did in times when he was homesick and feeling nostallgic in his famous poem, *The Lake Isle of Innisfree*. To quote from this poem, then I will also feel peace coming 'dropping slow'. My view will not be ordinary, but remain special and mine, in my 'heart's core'.

> Rounded off reasonably well – but the essay didn't address the question fully.

(770 words)

GRADE: H3

P = 21/30
C = 20/30
L = 21/30
M = 9/10

TOTAL = 71/100

EXAMINER'S COMMENT

- Narrow response to the essay title due to focusing mainly on 'the view'.

- At times, reads more like a descriptive essay (reducing the 'P' purpose mark).

- Examples of other 'things' that make you 'glow' needed to fully address the question.

- Some interesting observations (e.g. in paragraph 6).

- Drifted off the subject (e.g. in paragraph 7).

- Repetition and some awkward expression in places (paragraphs 2 and 8).

- Mechanical errors include 'proverbiel', 'experiances', 'absieiling' and 'nostallgic'.

CLASS/HOMEWORK ACTIVITY

Write a paragraph for inclusion in the above sample essay. Introduce a new topic that broadens the response to the title.

You may choose to write about any 'thing' which makes you 'glow' with excitement and happiness (e.g. a treasured possession, item of clothing, favourite treat, sport, music, memory, etc.).

Aim for around 120 words.

Personal Essay-Writing Skills

Learning aim: To sustain focus throughout the personal essay

NOTE

Examiners are likely to penalise personal essays that lose focus and read more like a short story, a descriptive essay or a speech.

SAMPLE PERSONAL ESSAY

Write a personal opinion essay on some of the changes you would like to see in the world today.

SEC MARKING GUIDELINES (PCLM)

P: Understanding of *purpose*

Address the question directly, making effective use of elements of personal writing, e.g. first-person narrative, reflective tone, use of authentic personal voice, personal anecdotes or observations, revealing personal insights, etc.

SAMPLE PERSONAL ESSAY ANSWER

'THE CHANGES I WOULD LIKE TO SEE.'

1. I dream of a world of peace and equality. Is that some sort of hippy-dippy dream? I often feel today that our hearts are made of stone. The sad eyes of children stare out as they did in previous times of conflict and war. People who's opinions differ from the current 'in' view are ruthlessly hounded and cancelled by those who disagree with them. So how can we bring about change? I think it's time for the silent majority to be silent no more.

> Strong introduction, setting out a clear personal viewpoint.

2. To google or not to google, that is the question. One of the downsides of the so-called information highway is that the ability to actually think for ourselves, reflect and to allow things to echo inside our mind is being lost. I really fear that the voice of calm is being drowned in a huge tsunami storm of endless information and data. We click constantly to yet another link. I would like to see a day in the week when people did not read texts, e-mails, blogs and TikTok. Let's bring in an old-fashioned rest day, like Sunday was once supposed to be. Even God rested on the so-called seventh day.

3. Wherever you are, you see everyone staring at screens, not looking at or talking to other people who are right next to them. 'I must know, I must answer.' There is a constant search for endless information via the small screen. What have we done? Where is the simple pleasure of just standing and staring? More and more information is not the key to happiness. It's what we do with information that counts more. We need space to think about that.

> Some interesting suggestions – but need a little more development.

4. When I first read about the smoking ban in Ireland, I was surprised that it actually worked, but the rest of the world is now following. We have all heard stories of how the best craic takes place in the smoking area. I even know a few girls who pretended they smoked, so they could join the cool people in the so-called fun smoking area outside. All the boring non-smokers stayed inside. Yet smokers are still staying at a quarter of the population despite all the anti-smoking campaigns. No point in telling a smoker that spending 20 quid a day on their habit is equivalent to puffing their way through the price of a round-the-world holiday.

5. I think the banks and supermarkets are making life hard for older people. Download that new app, use the new self-service lane. They embarass people like my gran when she went into her local bank. 'Do you want me to show you how to use the ATM?' said the assistant with name badge and clip board. 'No', says gran. 'I want to go to the counter.' 'But I will show you how to do it', insisted the bank worker. 'It's easy!' 'I want to talk to an actual person,' says my gran. 'So, I am going to the counter'.

> Dialogue adds realism to the personal references.

6. I would like to see so-called morning chat shows banned. The directors of these programmes turn them into a sort of freak show. 'But all human life is there, I hear you object.' I don't agree. They are as fake as their presenter's smiles and fake emotions. Director stake advantage of the unfortunate participants and the audience in the race for what? Truth? No, for ratings. Hypocrites!

7. The old TV comedy shows are also now out of favour. They are politically incorrect. Real truth used to be shown by fictitious characters in a funny story. But the soaps today are too busy pushing a message rather than giving the audience relatable characters who are overcoming hard times. Yet, one well-known actress I read about believes soaps reflect society. She says they highlight social issues. I don't think so. Everything ticks a box. A recent news poll found 90% of TV viewers thought soaps had gone far too woke.

> Lack of detailed evidence weakens the argument that modern soaps don't highlight social issues.

8. Would you actually believe that classic episodes of old soap shows like Coronation Street now come with a ridiculous contents warning because modern attitudes have changed about certain topics? Are we not to be trusted to form our own opinions about what we see?

9. I have chattered enough about the world out there losing it's way. My own world would be a place of peace and equality. It would offer space to think, time to enjoy everyday simple pleasures and freedom to form an opinion. My world would not be filled with senseless wars, 24/7 technology, polluting smokers and people constantly taking advantage of others. Do you want change? It's time to speak up.

> Reasonable attempt to round off the personal reflection. The final question invites a response from readers.

(770 words)

EXAMINER'S COMMENT

GRADE: H3

P = 24/30
C = 22/30
L = 23/30
M = 9/10

TOTAL = 78/100

- Solid overall response generally focused on changes.
- Loses focus slightly in paragraph 4.
- Interesting range of illustrations and personal anecdotes.
- Some points (e.g. in paragraphs 3 and 6) would benefit from more developed discussion.
- Lively conversational and reflective style engages the reader.
- Expression slightly repetitive and there are some mechanical errors ('who's', 'embarass', 'presenter's', 'equivalent','losing it's way').

CLASS/HOMEWORK ACTIVITY

Write a reflective paragraph about one change that you would like to see in Ireland today.

If you wish, you may base your response on any of the points raised in the above sample essay.

Aim for around 120 words.

PROMPT !

- Solution to the housing crisis
- No more social injustice and poverty
- Government seriously tackling climate change to help save the planet
- An alternative to the CAO points system
- The end of discrimination, racism and sexism

> *Don't let the noise of others' opinions drown out your own inner voice.*
> **Steve Jobs**

Learning aim: To analyse reflective personal essay writing skills

Effective personal essays focus on **describing** your thoughts and feelings about experiences – **and reflecting** on them.

- Aim to create a **vivid impression** of the experience or feeling.

- Try to **involve the reader** in sharing the experience or feeling you are describing.

- **Clarify the emotions** you felt – e.g. joy, excitement, fear, sorrow, etc. – or a combination of these.

- There should always be a **sense of reflection and development**. Think about how the experience has changed you or others.

- Consider **what you have learned** about yourself, how you have changed and what you could have done differently.

SAMPLE PERSONAL ESSAY

Write a personal essay in which you reflect on how uninteresting life would be without vibrant charismatic people who add joy and inspiration. In your essay, you may refer both to people whom you know and to celebrities.

MARKING SCHEME GUIDELINES

- **P:** Focus – a **personal essay,** in which candidates reflect on how uninteresting life would be without vibrant charismatic people who add joy and inspiration.

- Understanding of **genre** – the effective use of some elements of personal writing, e.g. first-person narrative, reflective tone, use of authentic personal voice, personal anecdotes or observations, revealing personal insights, etc.

SAMPLE PERSONAL ESSAY ANSWER

1. Monday morning blues! The raindrops drizzle down the window. Another boring bus journey to another boring school day! I often think that most of life is routine, dull and you guessed, boring! But now and again life throws up a colourful, charismatic character who amps things up, adds a kick and a fizz to life, least when you expect it.

> Atmospheric opening is engaging, inviting readers into the essay.

2. Here we go! Just round the corner of the Texaco Garage and here he is, as he always is, Tom from up the road. Tom left his home a couple of years ago after a family row. He spends his day sitting on edge of the low wall, wrapped up in his furry trapper hat, just his nose visible between the extra-long ear flaps. He sips greedily from his paper coffee cup. Well, you might wonder, what is so special about Tom from up the Road. During the recent global pandemic, Tom has kept up his daily post on the edge of the low wall as loyally and true as any sentinel guard. My nan used to say, 'See, it can't be all bad. We'll get through. Tom from up the road is still there.' We would laugh, but secretly I was glad he was always there, giving silent hope to us all during some very dark days!

> Very good use of vivid detailed description and personal anecdote.

3. As the bus bumps along I scroll down my phone to read about another inspirational figure who has given so much hope and joy, Johnny Sexton, the Irish rugby team's greatest all-time player. Whether his jersey was the blue of Leinster, the green of Ireland or the red of the Lions, Sexton delivered when it mattered most. Johnny's rousing battle cry to his Leinster team-mates when the team was under pressure really made all the difference. Reading about his competitive approach is inspirational. Not just to those interested in sport, but to people in general. The first Irish team captain to win a Grand Slam on home soil speaks directly to me. What a role model. Johnny always looks ahead and is confident about the future of Irish rugby. 'There's plenty more left in this team'. I find this type of inspirational attitude fires me up. I would really hope to be that kind of guy.

4. I reach into my schoolbag and pull out my history book – TEST TODAY! Michael Collins stares out confidently from the cover, dressed in his Irish army uniform. He controversially signed the Treaty which gave Ireland the freedom to achieve freedom. But he realised, 'I have signed my death warrant'. I think it's hard to stand up and do what you think is right when you know you will pay the penalty. Collins paid the ultimate price, gunned down in his own county by those who disagreed with what he had done. Today's cancel culture is harsh and cruel on those who go against its demands. I sometimes wonder could I have risked doing what Collins did. Yet if it wasn't for him, we would not have our country today. He was the 'Big Fella'.

> Viewpoint developed effectively with interesting portrayals from the world of Irish sport and history.

5. The bus has reached the school. The rain has stopped. We all hop out. A loud voice bellows, 'Here comes the sun, doo-doo-doo doo, Here comes the sun, and I say, It's alright!' We giggle and nudge each other. It's Johnny Who Sings. He spends his day singing at the top of his voice as he stomps along the streets. My Mam told me his speciality is to pop into the local hairdressers and serenade the curlered ladies, 'the smile's returning to their faces'. What a character. Johnny Who Sings brightens every day with his loud songs, delighting himself and extracting a smile from even the most tired face.

6. And now to the most truly extrovert character of all – 'Our Maureen', the awesome canteen lady! We give her a big salute as we pass by. Her tattooed arm waves back and the tattoos are truly awesome. She returned after last year's summer holidays with two grand worth of tats after a break up with her latest man, 'Toxic Bill'. At least that was the big rumour. The principal was outraged, but we thought it was just truly awesome. Go Maureen! When a nervous wee First Year queues for lunch, Maureen is the one who notices someone needs a little TLC. She heaps on an extra dollop of curried chips. 'Get that inside you!' she grins. The wee white face unscrunches a little. Good on you, Maureen!

> Essay builds to the lively description of the charismatic Maureen.

7. These colourful characters, some famous, some not, have brought me joy and inspiration on a dreary Monday morning's journey to school. I think people who think and act on the edge of life's normal routine bring happiness and hope. 'Living on the edge is risky but there is no fun living on the ground'.

> Confident conclusion to this very impressive reflective essay.

(800 words)

GRADE: H1

P = 28/30
C = 27/30
L = 26/30
M = 10/10

TOTAL = 91/100

EXAMINER'S COMMENT

- Bus journey provides a good structure for the writer's reflections.
- Effective use made of a range of illustrative characters.
- Interesting mix of famous figures and local people.
- More reflection on their longer term impact would be welcome.
- Engagingly personal and discursive tone, overall.
- Lively expression – apart from some awkward repetition in paragraphs 3 and 6.
- Organised focused response sustained throughout.

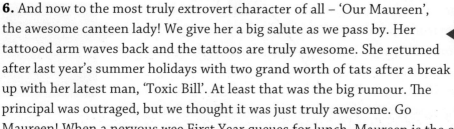

Close analysis of the above sample essay provides an understanding of some of the language skills needed for writing a successful personal essay.

- **Paragraph 1:** Short but effective introduction that **draws readers into the world of 'colourful' characters** who make the writer's life interesting. Good contrast between the dull image, 'raindrops drizzle', and the lively 'amps things up'.

- **Paragraph 2:** Descriptive details introduce the homeless man who survived throughout the pandemic's 'dark days'. The paragraph ends with some **brief reflection** about Tom's impact on the writer.

- **Paragraph 3:** Effective illustration making the point that role models, in sport and elsewhere, are **important inspirational figures**.

- **Paragraph 4:** Solid use of **historical reference** adds variety to the essay and offers scope for further personal reflection.

- **Paragraph 5:** Some good sequencing ('rain stopped') and lively portrayal of Johnny Who Sings. The writing has an easy **conversational fluency**.

- **Paragraph 6:** Lively paragraph, with another example of a larger-than-life character. Again, observations reveal a rounded, sympathetic figure. However, **the reflective element could be more developed**.

- **Paragraph 7:** Short overview **rounds off the essay** on the significance of individuals who add drama and excitement to life.

CLASS/HOMEWORK ACTIVITY

Write an introductory paragraph to a personal essay in which you reflect on the importance of having a sense of humour.

Aim for around 120 words.

- Briefly outline your views on why a sense of humour can be important.

- How is it useful in everyday life?

- Has it played a part in your relationship with family, friends or teachers?

- Are there any downsides?

Feature articles are written prose pieces which usually appear in magazines, newspapers and online.

They are much the same as **opinion pieces** (sometimes called **op-eds**, abbreviated from articles that are printed 'opposite the editorial page' in a newspaper).

While feature articles often **focus on human interest and lifestyle stories** in the news, they can be about any topic or issue.

The **style of these articles varies**. Some are balanced discussions or arguments, putting forward different views on a topic. Other pieces can be light-hearted and satirical.

The **aim of most feature articles is to inform, entertain and persuade**. They can also provide information or put forward new perspectives on current affairs.

Unlike a serious 'hard news' story, feature articles are generally seen as **'soft news'** and take a more personal look at modern-day life.

KEY CHARACTERISTICS OF FEATURE ARTICLES

- Prose pieces explore a topic or issue in the news.
- Writers' viewpoints combine facts and opinions.
- Personal, engaging tone, lively anecdotes
- Reflective and humorous touches
- Conversational, colloquial, emotive language
- Easily understood by readers.

ANALYSING A FEATURE ARTICLE

Read this extract from a newspaper feature article on 'The Cult of Celebrity', and briefly answer the four questions that follow.

THE CULT OF CELEBRITY

Today there are so many celebrities that I'm beginning to understand why they are called 'stars'. Not because of their dazzling brilliance but because of their sheer numbers! When ten-year olds are asked, 'What do you want to be when you grow up?', they answer, 'I want to be famous'. So why are we so obsessed with the rich and famous?

Some people are born famous, like royalty. Some achieve fame, such as film stars or musicians. Others have fame thrust upon them, like crime victims. Sometimes fame is short lived – but it can also last a lifetime. In rare cases, like Elvis Presley and Dolores O'Riordan, celebs can become timeless icons.

Whatever the causes or circumstances, being a celebrity changes your relationship with the world. You leave behind being a private person and become public property. Everybody wants to claim a bit of you. You are the object of envy as well as admiration – fair game for criticism, interrogation, ridicule and spite.

'We make 'em, we break 'em!'

1. **What is the purpose of the article?** Informing, persuading, discussing, reflecting, etc.

2. **Who is the target audience?** Age group, gender, status, interest, etc.

3. **What kind of language is used?** Informative, discursive, humorous, persuasive, etc.

4. **What is the tone of the piece?** Formal, serious, informal, comic, personal, etc.

POPULAR TYPES OF FEATURE ARTICLES

○ **Personality profiles**   ○ **Human-interest stories**   ○ **Discussing news issues**

CLASS/HOMEWORK ACTIVITY

Read the following opening paragraph from a magazine opinion piece titled 'In Praise of Sport', and answer the question that follows.

Sport has the power to revolutionise the community. Our own GAA is founded in 1884 in the Hayes Hotel in Co. Tipperary. Until then, only the gentry played sport in Ireland. Now sport was open to all. The GAA emphasises the non-payment of players. It relies on the efforts of volunteers. The organisation is family focused. Throughout rural and urban areas, young and old are welcome. The GAA has helped form a real sense of belonging among the widespread Irish diaspora on every continent of the world. GAA matches form a topic of conversation throughout the 32 counties of our divided island. Driving up a remote road in the heart of Donegal, the colours of the local club will be proudly displayed, hammered onto the gatepost or decorating a small bush. Sport is an important part of who we are, what we hold in common and where we have come from.

In your opinion, is this an effective opening that would entice you to read the full article? Give reasons for your answer, using reference to the text.

Aim for around 120 words.

PROMPT !

- Is the viewpoint clearly expressed?
- Are the arguments in favour of the GAA convincing?
- Is there anything you disagree with?
- Do you think the article is realistic? Or sentimental?
- What points of interest does the opening raise?

EFFECTIVE FEATURE ARTICLE INTRODUCTIONS

Some of these techniques can be used to capture the reader's initial interest:

- **Question** – If readers really want to know the answer, they'll read on.
- **Anecdote** – Personal stories or memories usually interest readers.
- **Quotes** – Catchy quotations are often used in personality profiles.
- **Action** – Begin at a dramatic moment that excites the reader's interest.
- **Description** – Absorbs the reader's attention with vivid details.
- **Shock/horror** – Sensationalism and humour can sometimes hook readers.

SAMPLE FEATURE ARTICLE

Write an article to be published in an online journal about what it means to be part of a 'global generation'. Your article may be serious or humorous or both.

MARKING SCHEME GUIDELINES

P: Focus on an article suitable for an online journal.

Understanding of **genre**:

- An article can be informative, reflective, entertaining, etc.
- The effective use of some journalistic elements is expected, e.g. an engaging writing style, clarity, inclusion of facts, opinion, analysis, personal observations and insights, etc.

SAMPLE ANSWER

1. I am part of today's Generation Z, the first truly global generation. We have been born into a more digitally interconnected reality than any generation before us. Is this good or bad?

Open question invites readers into the discussion.

2. Young people of my age have a very keen global awareness. Events happening half way around the world impact us in real time as if they occurred just down the road. The Titan submersible disaster and the huge search operation in the mid-Atlantic had us all on the edge of our seats. World-wide attention was caught in a real global conversation. It turned out that the wife of the CEO of the Ocean Gate sub was a great-great granddaughter of a wealthy woman who died in the original Titanic disaster. On April 15th, 1912, she had refused to leave her husband's side because he would not take a place in the lifeboats. Women and children were to be saved first. Instead she gave her lifeboat place and her fur coat to her maid! This is the global village, the new 'glocalism' where we feel connected to present and past events worldwide.

3. We global Gen Zers are extremely active online, not only for information. We are even called the digital natives because we have grown up with the new technology. This is where we work, shop, date and make friends, often spending maybe 6 hours a day online. We engage in global consumerism. We zip between sites, apps and social media feeds. We are particularly impacted by influencers on apps like Tik Tok. Gen Z makes up 60% of its over one billion users. We also visit distant corners of the internet where we can discuss our particular passions and interests with like-minded people who might not be in our own physical area.

> Expression could be more varied. 'We' over-used at the start of sentences.

4. Young global citizens like us are active campaigners on important issues like climate change and Make Poverty History. Unlike older people, we passionately believe in being 'world citizens'. We are aware that our individual actions can impact the whole world. We feel that we can be part of the solution. That's why we are prepared to raise our voices in online campaigns for change.

5. However, there is a serious downside to all of this awareness. A recent McKinsey consulting report revealed that Gen Zers have the least positive outlook of any generation. It stated that this generation feels overwhelmed by stress. global unrest, financial worries and climate anxiety. And then there's the long list of personal worries. We're constantly told that young people have always struggled with change, but there has just been so much of it in recent times – and Covid hasn't helped anyone. I just feel that the big world out there is much more scary than ever – and young people haven't actually got the experience to deal with it.

6. Self-identity or belonging is a very basic human need. We all want to be part of a community, family or group. Belonging leads to a sense of being valued and listened to. Gen Zers often try to gain social identity and acceptability by wearing brand names like Nike. But there can also be a problem with this. Often huge corporations sub-contract work to sweatshops for low wages and poor conditions simply to maximise their profits. Do we really want to gain an identity like this? Being a global citizen can be complicated.

> Good range of points develop the discussion, giving insights into the Gen Z reality.

7. We global citizens can look forward to unsettled working careers. Surveys show that we may change jobs up to ten times between the age of 18-34. The idea of a permanent job for 40 years with the same firm has almost become a thing of the past. But with its loss goes a sense of belonging, loyalty and security. Many of us so-called global citizens including myself worry about the future. Working with large multi-national companies often means short term contracts without health benefits or pension schemes. Change can be good, but as every gardener will tell you, a plant needs to put down roots to survive. Continuous uprooting prevents a plant from thriving. Is nature warning us?

> Effective balanced approach, looking at both positive and negative aspects.

8. Recent inventions like ChatGPT can also worry Gen Zers. What's to prevent a lazy student from obtaining a high grade in school or college thanks to ChatGPT? And how will the hard-working student be fairly rewarded? Apple are already advertising GPT-4 for iPhone. 'Get AI assistance for Homework' goes the ad. Then WikiHow is showing how to jailbreak ChatGPT content filters! So far, no filter has been developed to prove 100% whether an assignment was created with the help of ChatGPT. Will we have to return to depending totally on the old system of pen and paper in a written exam to get a fair result? We have yet to see how this will play out.

> Thought-provoking questions raised at the end of the article.

9. So, is being part of a global generation good or bad? Like everything in life, it is mixed. I think it is good that we desire an inclusive world which is tolerant of difference. But there seem to be more and more problems facing us. It will be interesting to see how Gen Zers will survive the challenges of being the first truly global generation.

(840 words)

EXAMINER'S COMMENT

GRADE: H1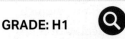

P =   30/30
C =   28/30
L =   26/30
M =   10/10

TOTAL = 94/100

- Sustained focused response exploring various aspects of the 'global generation'.
- Interesting observations on the impact of the global village and social media.
- Perceptive points about the negative impact of the global generation well-supported with topical references to news stories and statistics.
- Some well-developed commentary, e.g. on ChatGPT.
- Reflective, personal tone in paragraphs 5 and 7 is engaging.
- Note-like structure at times and some repetition of expression (paragraphs 3 and 4).

FEATURE WRITING ROUND-UP

- While the opening paragraph draws readers in, the conclusion should be written to help them remember the key opinions expressed.

- Wrap up the discussion – perhaps by briefly circling back to the opening.

- Keep it short and snappy, however. A long summary isn't the most creative way to end your article.

- An insightful question might be more memorable.

- Or maybe a strong image or interesting – even humorous – quote.

CLASS/HOMEWORK ACTIVITY

Write a paragraph for a feature article on your school website in which you give your views on how young people's fashion choices reveal their personalities.

Aim for around 120 words.

PROMPT !

- To what extent do young people use fashion to express themselves?
- Do clothes and image go hand in hand?
- Importance of designer brands?
- Impact of peer pressure, celebrities, influencers?

> We don't need to share the same opinions as others, but we need to be respectful.
>
> **Taylor Swift**

Learning aim: To understand key aspects of discursive language

DISCURSIVE WRITING

● Discursive writing uses the **language of argument** to examine a topic or issue.

● It takes a **balanced approach** that considers viewpoints both for and against a subject (arguments and counter-arguments).

● Discursive essays are **thought-provoking**. They aim to stimulate reflection, allowing readers to form their own views.

THE LANGUAGE OF ARGUMENT

● Discursive language is used in articles, speeches and opinion pieces.

● Discussions are logical – unlike persuasive speeches, which are based on emotion.

● The discursive tone is engaging and often inspiring.

● Points are based on reasonable evidence – facts, data, surveys, statistics, etc.

● All evidence should be realistic and verifiable (can be proven as true).

● Arguments are balanced, e.g.: 'School uniforms are criticised because they remove individuality, yet they also create a sense of belonging and pride'.

● Linking phrases are often used, e.g. 'however', 'therefore', 'on the other hand', etc.

ANALYSING DISCURSIVE WRITING

The following extract is from an edited BBC article about climate change.

CLIMATE CHANGE: HOW DO WE KNOW IT IS HAPPENING AND CAUSED BY HUMANS?

Scientists and politicians say we are facing a planetary crisis because of climate change.

But what's the evidence for global warming and how do we know it's being caused by humans?

HOW DO WE KNOW THE WORLD IS GETTING WARMER?

Our planet has been warming rapidly since the dawn of the Industrial Revolution. The average temperature at the Earth's surface has risen about 1.1C since 1850. These conclusions come from analyses of millions of measurements gathered in different parts of the world. The temperature readings are collected by weather stations on land, on sea and by satellites.

Multiple independent teams of scientists have reached the same result – a spike in temperatures coinciding with the onset of the industrial era. In fact, scientists estimate the Earth hasn't been this hot for about 125,000 years.

HOW DO WE KNOW HUMANS ARE RESPONSIBLE FOR GLOBAL WARMING?

Greenhouse gases – which trap the Sun's heat – are the crucial link between temperature rise and human activities. The most important is carbon dioxide (CO_2), because of its abundance in the atmosphere.

Burning fossil fuels and chopping down trees lead to the release of this greenhouse gas. Both activities exploded after the 19th Century, so it's unsurprising that atmospheric CO_2 increased over the same period.

WHAT IMPACT ARE HUMANS HAVING ON THE PLANET?

The level of heating Earth has experienced already is predicted to cause significant changes to the world around us.

- The Greenland and Antarctic ice sheets are melting rapidly.

- The number of weather-related disasters has increased by a factor of five over 50 years.

- Global sea levels rose 20cm (8ins) in the last century and are still rising.

- Since the 1800s, the oceans have become about 40% more acid, affecting marine life.

BUT WASN'T IT WARMER IN THE PAST?

There have been several hot periods during the Earth's past.

Around 92 million years ago, for example, temperatures were so high that there were no polar ice caps and crocodile-like creatures lived as far north as the Canadian Arctic.

That should not comfort anyone, however, because humans were not around. At times in the past, sea level was 25m (80ft) higher than the present. A rise of 5-8m (16-26ft) is considered enough to submerge most of the world's coastal cities.

There is abundant evidence for mass extinctions of life during these periods. And climate models suggest that, at times, the tropics could have become "dead zones", too hot for most species to survive.

For many years, groups of so-called climate "sceptics" have cast doubt on the scientific basis of global warming.

However, virtually all scientists who publish regularly in peer-reviewed journals now agree on the current causes of climate change.

Close analysis of this sample provides an understanding of some of the language skills needed for effective discursive writing.

- Headline is discursive, engaging the reader. It **questions climate change**, suggesting that there are arguments for and against.

- In the second paragraph, the phrase 'what's the evidence' emphasises the **logical approach** to the issue, based on facts.

- This is followed by **scientific data** based on 'temperature readings'.

- Four short bullet points provide **evidence of the negative impact of human activity** on the planet.

- The debate continues with **counter-arguments** based on 'several hot periods during the Earth's past' which indicate that global warming is exaggerated.

- Conclusion **supports the views of 'virtually all scientists'** over the 'so-called climate "sceptics"'.

SUGGESTED DISCURSIVE WRITING STRUCTURE

- Intro – attract reader's interest, introducing issue, possibly using quote or rhetorical question.

- Argument and initial evidence and proof, supporting the view expressed.

- Follow-up arguments and evidence and proof, opposing the view expressed.

- Conclusion – summarise arguments, state personal position, closing comments.

CLASS/HOMEWORK ACTIVITY

Write a discursive paragraph outlining your views on how your local town or community has responded to the issue of climate change.

Aim for around 120 words.

PROMPT !

- Do you have strong views on climate change? Or mixed feelings?

- Have any changes happened in your school? Are these useful or ineffective?

- Is your community involved in improving the local environment? Give some examples. Or are most people disinterested?

- Do you or your family look for sustainable alternatives to the products you buy?

> I write it because there is some lie that I want to expose.
>
> **George Orwell**

Learning aim: To write an effective discursive essay

- Discursive writing is about exploring particular topics in a balanced way.

- A discursive essay considers all sides of an argument, providing readers with objective evidence about a subject.

- The key aim of discursive essays is to convince readers that the arguments you are presenting are reasonable and valid, but allowing them to reach their own conclusions.

EFFECTIVE DISCURSIVE WRITING

- Key arguments are organised in **separate paragraphs**.

- A **topic sentence** in each paragraph highlights your point.

- **Linking words** connect arguments effectively.

- Each paragraph should have **well-developed ideas** supported by examples or references.

SAMPLE PLAN

1	Introduction
2	Argument: Point 1 + Evidence
3	Argument: Point 2 + Evidence
4	Argument: Point 3 + Evidence
5	Opposing Argument + Counter
6	Conclusion

GETTING STARTED

Always take time to plan the main points you wish to discuss in your essay.

Write a discursive essay about strong voices in modern society and discuss their effect on our lives.

In your response to this title, aim to get the reader's attention from the beginning by using an effective technique, such as:

- **Lively/provocative opening** – Why does every wrinkly old rock singer believe that we need to hear their comments on society's problems?

- **Balanced/objective introduction** – Strong voices in modern society can lift humanity to greater achievements or plunge them into violence and chaos.

- **Thought-provoking quotation** – The young Pakistani activist, Malala Yousafzai commented, 'When the whole world is silent, even one voice becomes powerful'.

- **Illustrative/revealing beginning** – On a drizzly Monday morning, Sean cowered in the bike shed, fearing that no one would ever speak up for him.

LINKING WORDS

Linking words and phrases show readers the development of your argument. They are often placed at the beginning of a new paragraph.

USEFUL LINKS

- Developing your points – similarly, in addition, for instance, etc.

- Contrasting ideas – however, on the other hand, etc.

- Making clear-cut statements – without question, absolutely, etc.

- Concluding/summarising – therefore, in brief, overall, etc.

TONE

For most discursive essays, it's best to write formally, avoiding slang and jargon, which would be unsuitable for a serious discussion.

CONCLUSION

- Summarise your central point. End on a strong decisive note, leaving readers interested in topic.

SAMPLE CONCLUDING PARAGRAPH

This is a sample conclusion for a discursive essay on the internet's role in education.

The internet has already had a dramatic positive influence on education. Teaching's future lies in the opportunities it offers for digital learning and worldwide communication. Of course, there are dangers – but the fact is that the internet is here to stay. Now is the time to focus on its potential for good.

SAMPLE DISCURSIVE ESSAY

Write a discursive essay for a popular magazine on the importance of independent thinking and its impact on today's world.

MARKING SCHEME GUIDELINES

P: Focus – a **discursive essay**, in which candidates discuss the importance of independent thinking and its impact on today's world.

Understanding of **genre** – the effective use of some elements of discursive writing, e.g. use of factual information, references, arguments and counter-arguments, consideration of a variety of views, opinions and personal experiences, illustrations, allusions, analysis, etc.

SAMPLE ANSWER

1. What is an independent thinker? Independent thinking simply means that you can think for yourself and not simply follow others. It also means being imaginative and creative. This important skill can bring success – in exams and work. I believe that thinking independently does not mean being stuck with one particular viewpoint, no matter how popular. It involves being willing to change your opinion.

> Clear introductory overview engages the interest of readers.

2. When I think of examples of well-known independent thinkers, the ones that come to mind stand out as leaders who are true to themselves. For example, the famous American inventor, Thomas Edison, is known as that guy who perfected the electric light bulb. It was Edison who said that Genius is 1% inspiration and 99% perspiration. From what I know about him, he learned most things by reading on his own. He was fascinated by technology and spent a lot of time making up experiments because he was a very curious child. During his teens, he saved a three-year old boy from a runaway train and the child's grateful father trained him as a telegraph operator. Edison asked to work the night shift so he could keep reading and experimenting. It's clear that independent people like him know exactly what they want.

3. Later in life, Edison invented the movie camera – an invention that has transformed our world. His film studio produced hundreds of movies including the first Frankenstein film. Edison was a free thinker who made things happen and set up the first industrial research lab. Way back in 1915 he stated that every woman in America was going to have the vote. He was proud of the fact that in the First World, he never invented weapons to kill, but worked on defensive weapons only. He believed that until we stop harming all other living beings, we are still savages. This man represents independent thinking by questioning authority and working to change things for the better.

> Developed portrayal of Edison effectively explores some key qualities of independent thinking.

4. In more recent times, another American who has totally revolutionised the way we live is Steve Jobs, co-founder of Apple Computers. Most people know that he founded Apple in 1976 and then left his company after a dispute and founded, Pixar, which produced the popular animated children's film, 'Toy Story'. When Apple was on the verge of bankruptcy. Steve returned and with his new advertising campaign, 'Think different', he launched the Apple Store, the iMac, iPod, iPhone and iTunes. Steve had problems at school and was pretty bored for a lot of the time. Life changed for him – but only when he got interested in study after one of his primary teachers bribed him to do his maths.

5. As everyone know knows, Jobs used independent thinking not only to succeed and change his own situation and the entire world for the better. He never stopped thinking outside the box. Even though he was terminally ill with cancer at the age of 57, he spent his time in hospital sketching new devices that would hold an iPad in a hospital bed. Like Thomas Edison, he refused to give in when facing unfavourable circumstances but chose to rise above them.

6. Dr Kathleen Lynn was another fiercely independent thinker like Edison and Jobs. At the age of 16, she became shocked by the disease and poverty she saw in the west of Ireland after the Famine, so she vowed to become a doctor. She was refused a job in Adelaide Hospital because she was a woman. She was involved in the votes for women movement. She was the chief medical officer during the 1916 Rising. When arrested she described herself as a doctor and a belligerent. Kathleen was strong-willed and set up St Ultan's Hospital for the mothers and children of the Dublin tenements. At that time the child mortality rate was worse here than in Calcutta in India. But Dr Lynn would not accept things as they were, but who battled, like Edison and Jobs to improve them.

> Good attempt at showing the common character traits of the three independently-minded public figures.

7. However, we must also be on our guard against some independent thinkers – especially those whose ideas lead to the destruction of society rather than the improving it. Notorious leaders like Hitler, Stalin, Pol Pot and others had new ways of thinking, but the result was misery for their people. These were power-hungry dictators who believed that society should follow their dictates or else be punished. China's Mao Zedong launched what he called the Great Leap Forward to develop his country from agriculture to industry. His country eventually became a dominant world power, but at a terrible human cost.

> Touched lightly on counter-arguments, but could have been more developed to broaden the scope of the essay. Expression is occasionally pedestrian and note-like.

8. In our global high-tech world, young people must think imaginatively and critically just like Edison, Jobs and Lynn. To be aware of modern problems like fake news, to deal with cyber-bullying and identity theft, we have to look carefully at what is going on and not to accept blindly what is just pushed forward. Question everything and listen to other people whose views are different. Just keep an open mind.

> Essay is rounded off well and addresses the reader at the end.

(830 words)

EXAMINER'S COMMENT

GRADE: H1

P =		28/30
C =		27/30
L =		26/30
M =		10/10

TOTAL = 91/100

- Focused very well on a number of independently-minded figures and their impact.

- Good use of factual background and biographical references.

- More of a discursive emphasis on what independent thinking is rather than pen portraits of historical figures needed.

- Interesting reflection on the contribution to society of three imaginative individuals.

- Some stilted expression and repetition – 'He' in paragraphs 2 and 4, 'She' in paragraph 6.

- Effective conclusion brings the discussion up to date.

CLASS/HOMEWORK ACTIVITY

Write the opening paragraph for a discursive essay about how public opinion today is affected by social media.

Aim for around 120 words.

PROMPT !

- What are the basic strengths and weaknesses of information found on social media?

- Does cancel culture play an important part in group discussion?

- Are celebrities' comments given too much importance?

- Is there enough emphasis on respect, tolerance and well-being of those with opposing views?

31 Using Descriptive Language

Learning aim: To discuss and analyse descriptive writing

- **Descriptive writing** engages readers. Its main purpose is to describe a person, place or thing in such a way that a vivid picture is formed in the reader's mind.

- Capturing an event through descriptive language involves **close attention to details** by using all five senses: sight, hearing, touch, taste and smell.

- The use of strong descriptive words – particularly adjectives and verbs – can also be effective, but only when **necessary and appropriate**.

- **Purple prose** is writing that is elaborate and long-winded. Trying to impress by using too many adjectives and **over-use of figurative language rarely works**. As a result, readers struggle to understand language that is flowery and melodramatic, for example:

> *Her hair was a cascade of shimmering gold, framing her delicate features like a halo of light, while her eyes shone like blue-green emeralds in the moonlight.*

When used effectively, good figurative writing stimulates the reader's senses, and is often more vibrant and interesting.

> *My task is, by the power of the written word, to make you hear, to make you feel — it is, before all, to make you see.*
>
> **Joseph Conrad**

NOTE

Literal language means exactly what it says while **figurative language** uses imagery and comparisons to describe something.

Metaphors are direct comparisons, e.g. 'Our next-door neighbour is a sly fox'.

A **simile** uses connecting words such as 'like' or 'as', e.g. 'Our next-door neighbour seems like a sly fox'.

SHOW ... DON'T TELL!

Effective descriptive language will **show and suggest** – and not just **tell**.

Telling:
I slowly began to get more and more tired as the long evening drew on.

Showing:
I leaned my head against the back of the old red armchair. The fire glowed and I felt my eyelids grow heavy as the room became dark and still. Then my eyes closed.

> The second example uses close observation and suggestion to involve readers. Visual and sound images help to create atmosphere.

APPEALING TO THE SENSES

Telling:

She drank water on a hot day.

Showing:

The cool water trickled slowly down her parched throat as the searing sun scorched her skin.

In the second example, 'parched' and 'scorched' refer to the senses, suggesting the powerful effect of the sweltering heat.

CLASS/HOMEWORK ACTIVITY 1

Read the following extract from *Holiday Memory* by Dylan Thomas, and answer the question that follows.

I remember the smell of sea and seaweed, wet flesh, wet hair, wet bathing-dresses, the warm smell as of a rabbity field after rain, the smell of pop[1] and splashed sunshades and toffee, the stable-and-straw smell of hot, tossed, tumbled, dug and trodden sand, the swill-and-gaslamp smell of Saturday night, though the sun shone strong, from the bellying beer-tents, the smell of the vinegar on shelled cockles, winkle-smell, shrimp-smell, the dripping-oily backstreet winter-smell of chips in newspapers, the smell of ships from the sundazed docks round the corner of the sandhills, the smell of the known and paddled-in sea moving, full of the drowned and herrings, out and away and beyond and further still towards the antipodes[2] that hung their koala-bears and Maoris,[3] kangaroos and boomerangs, upside down over the back of the stars. And the noise of the pummelling[4] Punch and Judy[5] falling, and a clock tolling or telling no time in the tenantless[6] town; now and again a bell from a lost tower or a train on the lines behind us clearing its throat, and always the hopeless, ravenous swearing and pleading of the gulls …

1. **soft drink**
2. **Australia and New Zealand**
3. **indigenous people**
4. **thumping**
5. **children's puppet show**
6. **deserted**

Comment briefly on two stylistic features of Dylan Thomas' descriptive language in the above extract. Support your answer with reference to the text.

CLASS/HOMEWORK ACTIVITY 2

Read the descriptive article below, and answer the question that follows. Support your answer with reference to the text.

The cars are belching out fumes. The air is foul. All around harsh beeping and engine revs assault my ears. The heavy rush hour Friday traffic bungs up the roads, stale and slow. I get on the Dart. Soon the traffic begins to ease as we reach Dun Laoghaire. The seagulls swirl, squawking loudly as they swoop for discarded chip bags. The grey light becomes luminous, dancing on the waves. The air smells sweeter, with a salty tang. Just ten minutes from Dublin's congested city centre the scene has changed utterly. A light show begins to play out. Soft pinks and peaches appear in the evening sky. Harsh engine sounds have given way to the soft waves, gently stroking the old sea walls.

Comment briefly on two qualities of the descriptive language in the above extract, supporting your answer with reference to the text.

PROMPT !

- What is your first impression?
- Sight, sound, smell, taste, texture, feeling?
- Which people or groups seem interesting?
- What buildings attract your attention?
- Any surprises? Anything unusual or funny?

If you want to be a writer, you must do two things above all others: read a lot and write a lot.

Stephen King

CLASS/HOMEWORK ACTIVITY

Write a descriptive paragraph (around 120 words) which captures everyday life in an Irish town from the viewpoint of an observant foreign visitor.

Learning aim: To write a vivid descriptive essay

> *Don't tell me the moon is shining; show me the glint of light on broken glass.*
>
> **Anton Chekov**

- Descriptive essay writing aims to **involve readers.**
- Its purpose is to describe a person, place or thing in detail so that **a clear impression** is formed in the reader's mind.
- **Atmosphere** is created through visual and sound images.
- **Detailed observation** invites readers to reflect on the significance of what is being described.

NOTE

A descriptive essay may contain other language genres (e.g. information, narration and the aesthetic use of language), but the focus should be placed on description.

SAMPLE DESCRIPTIVE ESSAY

Write a descriptive essay which captures night-time sights and sounds in your local town or village.

When you are describing
A shape, or sound, or tint
Don't strike the matter plainly
But put it in a hint;
And learn to look at all things,
With a sort of mental squint.

Lewis Carroll

MARKING SCHEME GUIDELINES

P: Focus – **a descriptive essay** which captures night-time sights and sounds in your local town or village.

Understanding of **genre** – the effective use of some elements of descriptive writing, e.g. imagery, setting, creation of atmosphere or mood, attention to detail, figurative language, appeal to the senses, etc.

SAMPLE ANSWER

1. Never again! The Basement disco lived up to its low name. Rotten night – and everyone had a partner except me! Am I glad to be out of that sweltering hell hole and into the night air! My docs beat out a sharp rhythm on the old cobbled path. The ground is shining darkly after another shower of rain. The silence is deep. I breathe in a huge gulp of cool evening air. The night air is scented with the early spring cherry trees, their soft petals in a swirl of pink. A very different scene from the heaving thick atmosphere of the disco.

> Opening focuses well on the contrasting sights and sounds inside and outside the disco.

2. Turning a corner, I look up at an open window. A couple appear against the bright yellow square. It's not a happy scene.

'I'm tellin' you, don't dare speak to me like that again!' screeches a female voice.

'Stop carryin' on like a spoilt baby!' a male voice growls.

'I've had it with you! That's the last insult you'll give me!'

3. A door slams. The front door is suddenly flung open and a sobbing figure in a hoodie appears. A black plastic bag plops from the open window onto the wet grass.

> Short burst of sharp dialogue bring the change of scene to life. Verbs ('slams' and 'yells') continue the emphasis on sounds.

'And don't bother comin' back!' he yells.

'I won't!'

The bag is picked up and she runs up the street. Couple paradise lost.

4. I walk on. The night city is a strange place, dimly lit by the new shadowy LED lights, eerily blue instead of the old comforting glow of orange. 'A big improvement to save the planet!' I used to like the warm orange light. So everything changes! A lone plastic bag hangs on a low hedge. It rustles in the gentle night breeze. Had it once kept a brightly coloured magazine of dreams for an exhausted commuter? Or had it held a collection of sweet nursery rhymes for someone's favourite grandchild? Perhaps it had been packed with books and copies for a bored student? Now abandoned, the bag shape rustles in the ghostly light. The last bus trundles past, carrying another group load of grey faced workers.

5. Suddenly my nostrils sense the sharp smells of curried chips and 'oniony' burgers. Just up ahead is the late-night chipper, 'Rocky Joe's'. Like a crowd of scavenging crows, groups of young people hang around the neon lit front. Boys jostle and push each other in the usual macho display for the giggling girls. Little screams come from the girls as they endlessly pull poses for the millionth selfie of the night. As I make my way past, a huge spray of beer erupts into the night air. As if on cue, one girl moves away from the group, swaying softly in the night air while the crowd sings along to the Taylor Swift hit, *Cause they said the end is coming. Everyone's up to something.* The phones click endlessly capturing the precious night time fun.

> Range of colourful illustrations adds interest. Details have a cinematic effect.

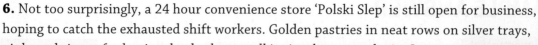

6. Not too surprisingly, a 24 hour convenience store 'Polski Slep' is still open for business, hoping to catch the exhausted shift workers. Golden pastries in neat rows on silver trays, pinky red rings of salami and pale cheeses all invite the passer-by in. I stare into the shop. Its neat little counter covered with boxes of smoked fish and the smiling owner standing close by. I wonder if the white-coated Polish owner later will stare at the moon, perhaps thinking of loved ones far away, hoping that they too are looking up. In a strange way, the curved moon is a channel of communication between those who left and those who stayed.

> Effective mix of descriptive aesthetic and reflective writing.

7. A black cat crosses my path. For luck? Its dark slinky shape slips effortlessly beneath the hedge, disappearing into the night air. The hunt for prey is on. A flickering strip light of a taxi passes, also on the hunt – but for a late-night fare. A group of noisy lads with green scarves and hats, carrying plastic cups of beer, spill out onto the steps of the pub. 'Olé, olé olé olé!' they sing as they argue about the missed penalty that would have saved the match.

> Realistic and closely observed description rounds off this impressive essay.

'He could have done it y'know!'

'He's well past his best, time to hang up the boots for good!'

'Will you look at who's talkin'!'

8. I quicken my steps. The city at night seems to be for the lost and the lonely. I pass by a huddled shape in a doorway under a mound of cardboard. Here are some of the city's outcasts, the homeless, the dispossessed. And there but for the grace of God – as my Nan would say. I'm thankful I have a home to go to. I push open my creaky gate and fit my key in the front door'.

(780 words)

GRADE: H1

P = 30/30
C = 28/30
L = 27/30
M = 10/10

TOTAL = 95/100

EXAMINER'S COMMENT

- Sustained focus on late-night urban sights and sounds.
- Well structured around the walk through the streets.
- Detailed description of atmospheric scenes engages readers.
- Effective use of figurative language, vivid imagery and vibrant dialogue.
- Some impressive descriptive flourishes – although a little overdone in paragraphs 1 and 4.
- Varied, controlled expression – apart from some repetition, e.g. 'night air'.

CLASS/HOMEWORK ACTIVITY

Write a paragraph (about 120 words) for inclusion in a descriptive essay, entitled, 'Wintertime in Ireland – the most distinctive time of year'.

PROMPT !

- Vivid winter scenes – at home, travelling, school, clothing, social activities.
- Positive impact of winter weather on lifestyles and moods.
- Coffee and hot chocolate by the fire.
- Natural beauty of landscape and coastline.

Instead of telling us a thing was 'terrible', describe it so that we'll be terrified.

C. S. Lewis

Learning aim: To write effective informative articles and essays

- The language of information **communicates facts** about a topic. It is generally used to instruct, advise and educate.

- This type of language is **commonly used**, particularly in reports, web pages, textbooks, instructions, guidebooks, journalism, flyers, reference books, etc.

- The language used should be **straightforward and coherent**.

- Effective informative essays usually **avoid technical terms** or jargon that may not be understand.

FEATURES OF INFORMATIVE WRITING

○ **Facts, statistics, data, supportive reference, sources**   ○ **Objective, unbiased approach**
○ **Sub-headings, bullet points, questions**   ○ **Written in the present tense and the third person**   ○ **Accurate information which keeps readers interested and engaged**
○ **Connectives – *therefore, because, resulting in*, etc.**

SUGGESTED STRUCTURE OF INFORMATION ARTICLES

- Clear opening

- General factual overview of topic

- More detailed specific details

- Short, logical conclusion

- Accessible, easy-to-read layout

NOTE

While your response to Leaving Cert 'Information' essay titles will, of course, be on using **informative language**, you are likely to also write in other genres, such as personal, discursive, descriptive, etc.

For example, you might be asked to write 'an informative and entertaining article about Ireland's film industry' or 'the text of a talk offering advice to students about earning money and giving your personal views on part-time work', etc.

INFORMATIVE WRITING SAMPLE

CLASS/HOMEWORK ACTIVITY

Read the following informative article about the Underground Railroad, and answer the question that follows.

WHAT WAS THE 'UNDERGROUND RAILROAD'?

During the era of slavery in America, the Underground Railroad was a secret network of routes which helped slaves escape from the southern plantations to freedom in the North, particularly Canada. The name 'Underground Railroad' was used metaphorically. It was not a working railroad, but it served a similar purpose. It transported people long distances. It ran through buildings, including private properties, bars, churches and businesses.

The name 'Underground railroad' came about because those who used it disappeared as if they had literally gone underground. Guides were known as 'conductors'. Hiding places were 'stations'. Escaping slaves were 'passengers'.

WHO WERE THE MAIN 'CONDUCTORS'?

Levi Coffin, was President of the Underground Railroad. His religious faith as a Quaker did not allow him to take part in slave ownership. He helped more than 2,000 slaves escape despite boycotts from his neighbours and many death threats.

The Puritan, **John Brown**, believed he was sent by God to strike the 'death blow' to slavery. His family home was part of the Underground Railroad. He freed 11 slaves from a Missouri plantation and took them 1500 miles to Canada and freedom. Brown risked his life and all his possessions to help those 11 people to freedom. He was hanged in 1859 for leading a slave rebellion at Harpers Ferry before the American Civil War.

The Methodist, **Harriet Tubman**, helped Brown plan his raid. She too was inspired by her religion to act. She was an escaped slave herself and became a 'conductor'. Tubman led 13 expeditions and saved 70 slaves. She was one of the most wanted conductors and 'never lost a passenger'. Huge rewards were posted for her capture.

Harriet Tubman

More than 30,000 slaves escaped to Canada via the Underground Railroad. Following the Union victory in the American Civil War, slavery was outlawed in 1865.

Identify two features of the language of information in the above extract and comment briefly on the effectiveness of each.

PROMPT!

- Impact of detailed facts in the opening paragraph.
- Was the extract informative about American history?
- Questions and sub-headings – helpful or not?
- Did you think the piece was impartial and unbiased?

SAMPLE INFORMATIVE ESSAY

Write an informative article, for your online school magazine, aimed at parents and guardians about the problem of peer pressure on today's teenagers. Your article should include useful information and helpful advice.

MARKING SCHEME GUIDELINES

P: Focus – an **informative article** for your online school magazine, aimed at parents and guardians about the problem of peer pressure on teenagers.

Understanding of **genre** – the information/advice may range widely from the practical to the personal. However, the essay should contain a sense of audience and a strong factual element, including the effective use of some elements of informative writing, e.g. relevant references, reputable studies, reports or statistics, supportive advice, etc.

SAMPLE ANSWER

1. 'Peer pressure' is really the influence other young people can have on how a teen thinks and acts. Positive peer pressure encourages the teen today to be confident with a good sense of identity and belonging. Negative peer pressure can push the young person to very destructive behaviour, such as alcohol abuse, cigarettes and drug abuse. Everything can suddenly change. Family and close friends can be pushed away because of arguements. Schoolwork also suffers.

> Informative opening. Good focus on the range of problems associated with negative peer pressure.

2. Teen peer pressure can also badly affect a person's mental wellbeing. Peer groups become far too important to the teen. The young person naturally begins to move away from the parent-child relationship and begins to discover their own independence and identity.

> Reasonable attempt to illustrate the point about encouraging new friendships.

3. So how should a parent or guardian guide the teen? Well, they can encourage friendships with other teens who are confident in themselves and who will help encourage this confidence in your teen. For example, Mary was feeling that she could not make friends in her class and had to eat her lunch on her own each day. Mary's Mum asked Jane's Mum who was in Mary's class and was in a wheelchair if Jane would like to come over for pizza. Jane was a confident girl who did not see her disability as a disability but that that was just the way things were. Jane did archery and when she came over she asked Mary if she would like to come with her and try this hobby. Now Mary has a new friend.

4. So what is the key thing to remember? I believe it's to reach out and make an effort. Teach the young person to say no to peer pressure. Prepare them with a reason. When offered a cigarette, they can just say. 'No, thanks, I'm trying to get on the football team and smoking won't help my chances'.

> Undeveloped point would be more effective if dealt with in greater detail.

5. Cyberbullying is the spiteful use of words or pictures online which is used to cause harm to a young person's well-being. Cyberbullying is usually done through social media. Naturally, Irish adults worry about their teen's safety. Only 1 in 10 young people confide in a trusted adult that they are the victim of cyberbullying. My younger brother, Paul was cyberbullied after he put up a photo of himself in his sunglasses and leather jacket. Luckily, we are best mates and he felt he could talk to me. I told him you just block anyone who is being nasty. You don't have to take it when they hand it out.

6. So how do you keep your teenager safe online? Well, I think parents can ensure your teen's social media accounts are set to private, only accepting friend requests from people they know in real life. Warn the young person about the danger of sharing important information online such as passwords, full name, address or number. Keep reminding the teen the internet is forever. So be very careful about privicy and posting photos online. Never share passwords. Make sure your teen knows how to block, delete or even report anyone who is posting disturbing or inappropriate things online.

> Some well-supported and worthwhile advice here for parents.

7. If your teen is being cyberbullied, really listen to the young person's concerns. It's important to take action. Don't make little of their worries to make them 'feel better'. For example, my Mum didn't take Paul's worries about being cyberbullied seriously at first and just tried to tell him it doesn't matter. That won't do. You have to take action, just as I said before. Block them! You can reassure the young person that there are trained people in every part of Ireland who can offer help and support, such as the e-Safety guide.

8. Cyberbullying leads to poor attendance at school and performance then in exams. It causes teenage stress, often loss of confidence and even sometimes depression. Just because you, the experienced adult, have been very good at school, your teen mightn't find it every bit as easy as you yourself did. Understand that realising a teen's own potenntial, not just what you would like them to be, is needed. This is how you reduce pressure on your teen. It is their life, not yours.

> Awkward expression and repetition reduce the effectiveness of the discussion points at times.

9. Many young people experience terrible sadness at the break-up of a close personal friendship and feel that there will never be another person like that for them. But it doesn't help very much if the adult had went to the trouble of being helpful at first, but then laughs off the break-up with statements like 'There are plenty more fish in the sea' or 'You were far too good for them, anyway'.

10. Adults need to help the young person to manage their time, not to leave homework to the night before it is due. They can create a gentle routine before bed so that the young person goes off to bed relaxed and calm. Most important of all, listen carefully to understand the teen's stress and take their feelings seriously. The most basic thing is to help them work out what's within their control to change and what isn't.

> Summary of concluding tips and advice rounds off the essay well.

(830 words)

GRADE: H2

P =   26/30
C =   25/30
L =   23/30
M =   9/10

TOTAL = 83/100

- Effective opening introduces the subject of peer pressure.

- Informative approach to various aspects of the issue and offering some useful advice.

- Overall structure could be more organised to avoid repetition and random, undeveloped references (e.g. paragraph 9).

- Use of questions, headings and anecdotes reflects awareness of parent/guardian audience.

- Uneven expression – reasonably controlled, but repetitive and note-like at times (e.g. in paragraphs 6 and 7).

- Some mechanical errors ('arguements', 'privicy'. 'potenntial', 'had went').

CLASS/HOMEWORK ACTIVITY

Write an informative paragraph (around 120 words) outlining the value and importance of studying History as a Leaving Cert subject.

PROMPT

- Provides an understanding of the process of change over time.
- Opens students' minds to other cultures.
- Gives individuals a greater sense of identity.
- Enables individuals to develop their critical thinking.
- Offers insights into Irish social and political history.

> Knowledge is power.
> Information is liberating.
>
> **Kofi Annan**

Learning aim: To write a persuasive speech

- Speeches use both the language of **persuasion** and the language of **argument** to make an impact on listeners or readers. While argument relies on a balanced and reasonable approach, **persuasion appeals more to the audience's emotions.**

- The language of persuasion is **used widely** – in school debates, political speeches, press releases, advertising, propaganda and in some forms of journalism.

> *Speech is power, speech is to persuade, to convert, to compel.*
>
> **Ralph Waldo Emerson**

WORD POWER

- A **persuasive speech is intended to convince** the audience to do something – stop littering, buy something, change their minds about an important issue – so the speech must be crafted to suit a particular audience.

- Persuasive language is often **dramatic**. It appeals to **the emotions** and imagination of the audience in a way that is designed to get their sympathy and support.

- It's essential to **use the appropriate genre** when responding to Composing titles.

- Persuasive essays are unlikely to expect mere persuasion throughout, but the **persuasive element should play a significant part**.

- As with all other compositions, you will be including **language from several genres**, such as description, information, narration, etc.

SOME FEATURES OF PERSUASIVE LANGUAGE

- **An engaging tone** (personal, inspirational)
- **Flattery –** 'This intelligent audience is aware that I am absolutely right.'
- **Use of supportive evidence** (references, statistics, anecdotes)
- **Emotive language –** 'Our oceans are under fierce attack due to careless human behaviour.'
- **Emphatic style** (strong rhythm, repetition, exaggeration, memorable phrases)
- **Compelling rhetorical questions –** 'Who doesn't want to be successful in life?'
- **Involve the audience –** 'You must surely agree that we all need to act now.'
- **Engaging humour –** e.g. 'I can resist everything except temptation.' (Oscar Wilde)
- **Manipulation through fear –** 'Planet Earth will simply not survive more pollution.'

SAMPLE SPEECH

Write a speech, to be delivered to a youth conference on education for young people, about the key skills and knowledge that you think young people will need to succeed in the twenty-first century.

MARKING SCHEME GUIDELINES

P: Focus on **a speech** suitable for a youth conference on education in which you outline the key skills and knowledge that you think young people will need to succeed in the 21st century.

Understanding of **genre**:

● A speech can be informative, persuasive, reflective, entertaining, etc.

● The effective use of some elements of speech-writing, e.g. use of references, persuasive language, rhetorical style, personal anecdotes, emotive or inclusive tone, awareness of audience, etc.

SAMPLE ANSWER

1. I think young people have good skills and key knowledge that they need to suceed. No one knows what kind of future there's going to be. Sometimes I think it's going to be great, full of new inventions and people looking after the planet. Other times I think adults are just getting worse and worse and that the earth will soon be ruined by us humans because we don't realise how serious it is for us to look after the planet. But young people understand that the planet is in danger.

> Opening includes random comments – instead of directly addressing skills needed for the future.

2. I think another point is young people today have great ideas and plans. But they are often bored. They spend a lot of time on their social media and gaming. Tik tok, snapchat, facebook, instagram are some of the places they spend a lot of time. They also use Wiki and AI to help with homework and why not? This is all progress. Old people used to use libraries in their school days. What's the difference? But I don't agree with adults who think that the internet is the cause of all evil in the world. I think the internet connects young people with other young people all over.

> Drifts off the point, referring to boredom.

3. This makes the young teenagers less likely to be racist because they have being in contact with all sorts of people in different countries, so, I think this talent of the young person on the internet should not be looked down on. But it should be admired because it can stop them from becoming racist. It opens them to different ways of looking at things because a young person in another country will have a completely different life than the young person here in Ireland has, so that opens the mind of the young Irish person to look at things with different eyes. I think we will be not so narrow-minded and will end racism.

4. Young people are very keen on looking after the planet. We only have to look at all the protests they take part in, even online. This is a great skill because it means that they are not selfish and burnt up like the adults. The young teens still have hope, not like the adults. I don't think all knowledge comes from books, either like the adults think. Some books is full of fake news and the writers can have a hidden purpose that's being pushed. Just because it is in a book doesn't mean it's true.

> Good enough point – but could have been expressed more clearly.

5. I think what young people need is more exploring on your own on the internet to see what is being said. It's like a big libary at the touch of a screen. You can dip in and look at thing s for yourself. Adults say how do you know what you find on the internet is true? I would like to ask these adults how do you know what's in papers is true? And we have better skills and education than people nowadays.

6. Young people are a lot more savvy with technology than adults. This is a thing that is the key to improving the future. You often hear grandads dissapproving and saying that computers should come with an eight year old kid in the box. They mean that old people don't know how to use the new technology while the young person is completely good at it. Instead, the adults want to hold on to paper. They say things like you never know when those machines will break down, so then what?

7. Young people welcome technology and after all the future is going be full of advanced machines, like it or not. Just think AI. We are far better educated now. You can see in the supermarkets today with old people still fumbling with paper money. They pull out notes, then can't find their value card, then their paper voucher is out of date. Young people have all this on their smartphone. They quickly go through the checkout as a result which will be needed even more in the future.

> Drifts into further criticism of older people. More control of language needed.

8. Old people often say you can't beat experiance. I say you can. They are always on about been careful of everything. You hear less young people saying this. They just kind of go for it and see what happens. I think you need to do this to succeed in the future rather than being afraid to take a chance. Their won't be any progress if we keep being afraid to try new things.

9. Summing up my speech, I think young people are full of new ideas, full of looking after the planet. They are great on the internet and technology. They're not afraid and are full of energy. That's why I think these are the skills and knowledge that are going to be needed to suceed in the future.

> Attempts to sum up main points and round off speech.

(800 words)

EXAMINER'S COMMENT

- Uneven mid-grade response requiring much more focus.
- Some potentially good points on tech skills, racism and pollution.
- Arguments need to be more developed and supported by persuasive evidence.
- Little awareness of addressing an audience.
- Expression is repetitive and awkward in places (paragraphs 4 and 8).
- Mechanical errors ('suceed', 'being', 'is full', "experiance', 'libary', 'Their', 'dissapproving', 'less young', 'been').

GRADE: H4

P =   18/30
C =   17/30
L =   17/30
M =   8/10

TOTAL = 60/100

SUCCESSFUL SPEECH-WRITING

HOW DO I WRITE A GOOD INTRODUCTION?

Engage your listeners from the start. Make them aware of your viewpoint and let them know briefly what you will be speaking about.

Aim to get the attention of your listeners with the **opening sentence**. Think of it as a hook, drawing them in. A lively quotation, definition or curious fact can be effective. Short dramatic questions can also be useful.

CLASS/HOMEWORK ACTIVITY

Write your own introductory paragraph to the sample speech above, outlining the main points you will be addressing.

Aim for around 120 words.

PROMPT

- Briefly introduce yourself to the audience.
- Outline the key topics that that you plan to discuss.
- Focus on young people and the skills they will need in the future.
- Choose subjects you think will be important in the future.
- These might include global issues (world poverty, peace, climate).
- You may focus on personal concerns (e.g. education, work, housing).

- Speeches use both the language of **persuasion** and the language of **argument** to make an impact on listeners or readers.

- While argument relies on a rational, logical approach, **persuasion is usually more forceful** and often appeals to the audience's emotions.

- A **persuasive speech** is intended to convince the audience to do something – vote, stop littering, change their minds about an important issue.

- Persuasive writing is often **dramatic** – feelings, images and words are shaped to affect the imagination of the audience and get their agreement and support.

- The **language of persuasion is used widely** in school debates, political speeches, public relations' press releases, advertising, propaganda and in some forms of journalism.

SOME FEATURES OF PERSUASIVE LANGUAGE

- **Compelling tone** (intimate, inspirational, emotive, flattering, etc.) ○ **Supportive evidence** (anecdotes, illustrations) ○ **Strong rhythm** (repetition, memorable phrases) ○ **Rhetorical questions** ○ **Humour** ○ **Emphatic word choice**

NOTE

Leaving Cert speech essays are unlikely to expect persuasive writing throughout. However, **the persuasive element should play a significant part**. As with all compositions, you will be including language from several genres, such as information, narration, description, etc.

SAMPLE PERSUASIVE WRITING QUESTION

Identify two features of persuasive language use in the following paragraph and comment briefly on the effectiveness of each.

Aim for around 120 words.

OPENING OF PERSUASIVE SPEECH IN PRAISE OF TECHNOLOGY

Where would you be without your smartphone? Just think about it. Technology plays an absolutely huge part of our lives today. Like all technology, of course, there are some risks and dangers. But I want to argue the positive side. And there's loads of benefits. For a start, our phones keep us closely connected to our family and friends – and that means support when we need it.

Communication has never been quicker. And think of how much time we depend on texting, calls and social media. Thanks to our phones, we can set reminders that save us remembering all the things we have to do every day. So how does technology help us? Well, we use it in countless ways – from preparing our food to travelling around and keeping us entertained. How could we ever cope without technology?

SAMPLE ANSWER 1

I think there is good persuasive language in this opening debate speech in praise of technology. But nothing at all about the dangers which is a big problem. The list of the benefits and advantages of mobiles was also good. Another piece of persuasive language for the debate topic. This was about how mobiles keep us connected to our family and friends and that means support when we need it. There's also a lot of questions asked. I agree with what it says through the paragraph. Mobiles are the technology we all use when we're travelling around and they keep us entertained also. It's good persuasive language because it's the truth from the very start to the finish.

EXAMINER'S COMMENT

- This mid-grade response identifies persuasive features (e.g. strong arguments and questions).
- Very little follow-up discussion about their impact.
- Some of the points are copied directly from the paragraph.
- Less repetition and more fluent expression would have improved the answer.

SAMPLE ANSWER 2

This persuasive speech begins and ends with rhetorical questions that get the listeners thinking. Once the audience is involved, the speaker will have their interest and agreement. The language is clear and introduces the viewpoint very confidently, presenting 'the positive side' of technology. There are relatable examples that show how young people love their smartphones. For instance, using reminders and notifications which reduce stress. This would convince the audience right away. A final persuasive quality was exaggeration. Phrases such as 'absolutely huge part' and 'countless ways' are over the top but they add emphasis to the speech.

EXAMINER'S COMMENT

- Addresses both aspects of the question (persuasive features and their effectiveness).
- Engages closely with the emphatic language.
- Discussion points about the persuasive style are developed clearly.
- For example, rhetorical questions involve the audience.
- Expression is controlled throughout. Top-grade standard.

SAMPLE PERSUASIVE SPEECH

Write a persuasive speech for or against the motion: Language is a powerful weapon.

MARKING SCHEME GUIDELINES

P: Focus – a **speech** in which you argue for or against the motion: that language is a powerful weapon.

Understanding of **genre** – the effective use of some elements of speech-writing, e.g. use of references, persuasive language, rhetorical style, anecdotes, imagery, illustrations, inclusive language, awareness of audience, etc.

SAMPLE ANSWER

1. Adjudicator, members of the audience. We humans are the only species on the planet who communicate through speaking. Our history and our culture depend on our language. Irish people are shaped by the stories they tell. But language can be both a barrier and a bridge. It can divide, separate or join and unite. It is an arm which can comfort or hurt.

> Formal debate opening. Purposeful focus on the power of language. Good sense of audience.

2. I was slightly shocked to learn in my history class how some countries used language as a powerful weapon. When a country is colonised or occupied, the native language is suppressed. The language of the invader has a huge effect. The original culture is replaced. The old literature is conquered. So what is the message? The language of the conqueror is a weapon used to push down the native people.

> Emphatic, persuasive style, developing the argument effectively.

3. History can teach us a lot. Imagine this! Suppose for a moment that the Spanish had succeeded in taking over England when Elizabeth I was on the throne. As a result, Spanish is the main language in England. So imagine a world with no English literature. No Shakespeare! Everyday phrases which are in common use would disappear – 'he has eaten me out of house and home', 'the world's my oyster', 'vanish into thin air'.

4. England invaded Ireland for over 700 years. The English suppressed the speaking of Irish. This suppression of the native language was used as a weapon to try to destroy Irish culture. In the 1960s Algeria won independence from France. France had, like the English, used their language as the highest language in the land. Then Algerians put Arabic back into the schools to let the people get to know their language and culture. All showing that language is the weapon of defence for a people who want to keep their unique identity.

> Impressive references from history and literature in support of viewpoint.

5. The power of language can be seen in fairy stories which have been passed down for centuries. I like that our ancestors used stories to warn us of the dangers of doing wrong and abusing power. I like the story of Snow White. There has been a massive row recently because Disney Movies has tried to modernise the story. Language was used as a weapon to cut down those who didn't like how the story was changed. It goes to show how language can be such a powerful weapon.

6. Of course, language can also hurt personally. I don't agree with the old childhood rhyme, 'Sticks and stones may break my bones, but words shall never hurt me'. Do you? This rhyme is supposed to help the victim remain calm and not to get upset with bullying. I actually think verbal bullying, particularly online, is much more destructive than a physical fight. Online bullying has driven many teenagers to suicide. A recent study revealed that girls retreat into silence when confronted with online bullying. Hate speech is an offence here in Ireland when it is committed online. More evidence that language can seriously wound a person.

7. Don't you think we need to remind young people to protect themselves from this negative power of language? Remember this – the internet does not forget. Posts and messages can never be permanently deleted. Even Snapchat can be screen-grabbed. So don't post when angry. Keep your passwords and PIN numbers to yourself. Tell someone if you are being cyberbullied. And don't forget, you can always switch off.

8. Yet, language can be a force for good. South Africa's great freedom fighter Nelson Mandela once said, 'If you talk to a man in a language he understands, that goes to his head. If you talk to him in his own language, that goes to his heart'. Aren't we delighted when tourists coming here bother to learn a cúpla focail in Irish. We smile when the visitor tries out 'Conas atá tu?' This is the positive power of language, acting as a bridge, connecting people rather than hurting them.

> Emotive approach adds power to the compelling speech.

9. Language can also be used as a weapon to shut down free speech.
We all agree that debate and disagreement is necessary for a real democracy to work well. Cancel culture has now become part of the language we use in our lives. If someone becomes offended at another's opinion, a viral attack can break out on social media. People become hypnotized by slogans. Group think takes over. The result can be shattering for the victim. Isn't it shocking that people's good names and even jobs can be destroyed? Language is often the first weapon drawn in a fight. It is used to cut down the opposition.

10. The pandemic lockdowns really showed how powerful language could be. It was used as a link, a bridge to connect and support. People physically cut off from each other, connected through speech on Facetime and Skype. We chatted, we laughed, we sobbed. WhatsApp instant messaging offered group support.

> Short sentences, forceful language and questions make an impact.

11. I'd like to end with these two images. A parent quietens a crying baby by gentle lullabies. A warrior dashes into battle with a blood-curdling cry. And when you think of these two scenes, you realize that we must use language well. Language has hidden power, like a moon on the tides. Thank you for listening.

> Strong ending sums up the central argument and rounds off the speech successfully.

(860 words)

EXAMINER'S COMMENT

GRADE: H1

P =   28/30
C =   27/30
L =   28/30
M =   10/10

TOTAL = 93/100

- Well sustained, confident and compelling speech.

- Range of strong references to history, culture, bullying group thinking and the pandemic.

- Paragraph 5 more discursive than persuasive – and points needed more development.

- Good use made of persuasive elements (illustrations, repetition, emphatic speech rhythms and questions).

- Expression is varied and well controlled, overall.

CLASS/HOMEWORK ACTIVITY

Write the opening paragraph of a persuasive speech promoting the strengths of Ireland's second-level education system.

Aim for around 120 words.

PROMPT

- What are the basic strengths and weaknesses of the secondary education system?

- Does Transition Year offer a worthwhile alternative programme prioritising life and work skills?

- Are school exams based on equal opportunity? Do they encourage learning?

- Is there sufficient emphasis on respect, tolerance and well-being?

Learning aim: To understand some basic elements of narrative writing

Narrative writing includes a number of basic elements, such as:

- Plot
- Setting
- Character
- Conflict/Tension
- Resolution

PLOT

The plot is **what happens** in a short story. This usually involves a series of events that drives the narrative forward.

Essentially, **stories have three basic stages**: a beginning, middle and end.

The **beginning** introduces characters and sets up the conflict. In the **middle** section, the plot develops and reaches its high point or climax. The conflict is usually resolved in the **end**.

A good storyline traces cause and effect, involving readers in the sequence of events.

Plot *is not* the same as a story summary.

The King died and then the queen died is a story. The King died, and then the queen died of grief, is a plot.

E. M. Forster

SHAPING A SHORT STORY PLOT

While there are many different narrative structures, stories are often shaped as follows:

BEGINNING

Introduce your central character (or characters) and their world. What do they want to achieve? What challenges stand in their way? Remember, **there is no story without some kind of conflict or tension**. This can be between characters or between a character and his world. Inner conflict, i.e. tensions within a character's own mind, is also common.

PLOT DEVELOPMENT

What's going to happen? How will you build up to the confrontation or climax? The character must have a challenge and there should be an element of risk to keep the story exciting.

CLIMAX

The high point or climax refers to the main event or **turning point** in a story. The central character will have to make an important decision.

ENDING

The ending should make sense within the 'world' of the story. Conclusions usually resolve the conflict – either happily or unhappily. The main character has probably learnt a lesson about life or perhaps there has been an unexpected outcome. Some resolutions can be open-ended – a cliff hanger – leaving the reader to decide what might happen.

FLASHBACK

A story does not have to be told chronologically, i.e. the order in which key events occurred. A writer can choose to begin the story when the central character is already experiencing conflict, and then goes **back in time to** show how the character became involved in this predicament. This narrative device is known as flashback.

SHORT STORY OPENINGS

A good first line invites readers into the 'new reality' of a story. Opening lines often introduce the central character as well as the setting. They usually establish the start of the main plot – particularly if there is some hint of tension or conflict.

A character in mid-action is likely to capture the reader's interest. Decide whether you want your story to be comfortable or uneasy. What is the time of day, the weather, the mood?

An intriguing opening will make the reader want to read on.

> I snuggled happily under the warm duvet. Leaving Cert done and dusted, parents on holiday, the house entirely to myself, life was good. A faint noise sounded from the hall downstairs. Just the wind, I thought as I turned over. But there it was again, a steady series of creaks coming nearer, moving up the stairs …

The reader is engaged. Who is on the stairs? **What is going to happen next?** Will there be a robbery – or worse?

Always aim to make the opening interesting. It is best to involve readers through suggestion, rather than explaining everything.

> One day, Mark walked along the road towards Linda's house. He was hoping he might get a chance to see her. What he really wanted was that that she would just take some interest in him.

The writer is 'telling' the story rather than 'showing' it. How could it be improved?

> The road stretched endlessly in front of Mark on yet another cold autumn evening. Freezing wind stung his face. He pushed his hands deeper into his jacket pockets as he wondered if he might catch even a quick glimpse of Linda's house through the driving rain.

Notice how the writer is setting the scene – using the weather to reflect Mark's gloomy mood. Strong verbs ('stretched', 'stung') suggest his hopes and fears.

CLASS/HOMEWORK ACTIVITY

Read the following short story opening and write a short paragraph (around 100 words) commenting on any narrative features which you thought made it effective.

> There were no lights in the bike shed. The surrounding bushes loomed menacingly in the November twilight. A slight rustling came from the left corner. For an instant, Jack caught a blurred movement from the corner of his eye. He turned, breathing harder, and there it was … a small white hand parted the bushes. Jack turned quickly …

PROMPT

!

- What impression is created by the short opening sentence?
- Impact of 'loomed menacingly' and 'slight rustling'?
- How is the sense of developing tension suggested?
- Why is the image of the 'small white hand' intriguing?

NOTE

- The opening of a story should **get readers involved**, asking questions.
- It usually introduces the main character and the **hint of conflict**.
- The writer will often create an **atmosphere,** either relaxed or uneasy.
- Good stories have **believable worlds** where the events develop in interesting settings.

INTERESTING OPENING LINES

When I was a young lad twenty or thirty or forty years ago I lived in a small town where they were all after me on account of what I done on Mrs Nugent.

The Butcher Boy
Patrick McCabe

I write this sitting in the kitchen sink.

I Capture the Castle
Dodie Smith

It was a bright cold day in April, and the clocks were striking thirteen.

1984
George Orwell

If you really want to hear about it, the first thing you'll probably want to know is where I was born, and what my lousy childhood was like, and how my parents were occupied and all before they had me, and all that David Copperfield kind of crap, but I don't feel like going into it, if you want to know the truth.

The Catcher in the Rye
J.D. Salinger

In the beginning, the universe was created. This has made a lot of people very angry and been widely regarded as a bad move.

The Restaurant at the End of the Universe
Douglas Adams

It is a truth universally acknowledged, that a single man in possession of a good fortune must be in want of a wife.

Pride and Prejudice
Jane Austen

My name is Mary Katherine Blackwood. I am eighteen years old, and I live with my sister Constance. I have often thought that with any luck at all, I could have been born a werewolf.

We Have Always Lived in the Castle
Shirley Jackson

As a boy, I wanted to be a train.

Machine Man
Max Barry

If you are interested in stories with happy endings, you would be better off reading some other book. In this book, not only is there no happy ending, there is no happy beginning and very few happy things in the middle.

A Series of Unfortunate Events
Lemony Snicket

Once upon a time and a very good time it was there was a moocow coming down along the road and this moocow that was coming down along the road met a nicens little boy named baby tuckoo.

A Portrait of the Artist as a Young Man
James Joyce

Having placed in my mouth sufficient bread for three minutes' chewing, I withdrew my powers of sensual perception and retired into the privacy of my mind, my eyes and face assuming a vacant and preoccupied expression.

At Swim-Two-Birds
Flann O'Brien

As Gregor Samsa awoke one morning from uneasy dreams he found himself transformed in his bed into a gigantic insect.

The Metamorphosis
Franz Kafka

For the better part of my childhood, my professional aspirations were simple – I wanted to be an intergalactic princess.

Seven Up
Janet Evanovich

It was the best of times, it was the worst of times.

A Tale of Two Cities
Charles Dickens

Mr and Mrs Dursley, of number four Privet Drive, were proud to say that they were perfectly normal, thank you very much.

Harry Potter and the Philosopher's Stone
J. K. Rowling

CLASS/HOMEWORK ACTIVITY

Which of the opening lines to stories appealed to you most? Write a short paragraph (around 100 words) explaining your choice.

PROMPT !

- What was your initial reaction to the opening line?
- Did it surprise you? Raise questions? Feel creepy? Make you smile?
- Why would you like to read on?
- How do you think the story is likely to end?

Sample Story 1

Learning aim: To recognise narrative writing features in a sample story

CONFLICT AND TENSION

● **Conflict** usually involves a disagreement or disputes that characters have with someone or something outside of themselves.

● **Tension** is closely associated with conflict. It generally refers to simmering unease that threatens to develop into open conflict.

● **Inner conflict** is when characters try to deal with forces within themselves – secret fears, stress, self-doubts, etc.

> *I've been in a long and happy relationship for 22 years and it's never inspired me to write anything. It's too good – nothing to say. Problems, conflict, that's what makes for good stories.*
>
> **Emma Donoghue**

● **Without conflict or tension, there is no drama**. Every good narrative has a challenge or an issue that needs to be sorted – and that's where conflict comes in.

● Conflict is what **creates excitement and suspense**. It makes readers care about the story's characters and the eventual outcome.

PLANNING YOUR SHORT STORY

● **Your central character** might be **faced with a challenge** or confrontation involving another character – maybe a close friend or sometimes a complete stranger.

● The **struggle may be with someone in authority** – parents or guardians, school, work, the gardai, etc.

● A character might be struggling with **other forces,** such as technology or nature or even the supernatural.

REMEMBER

No problem? No story!

SETTING

Fiction has various key elements, including setting, plot and characterisation. The setting is **where and when the action takes place**. The writer creates a 'new reality' that the reader enters and then takes for granted while the story and characters become more believable.

Setting provides the **framework of the narrative**, allowing it to develop in a particular direction. Every story would change significantly if the characters and plot were suddenly moved to another time and location.

Setting often **shapes the opening atmosphere** of the story. It can also show the passing of time through descriptions of the weather, lighting, season, etc.

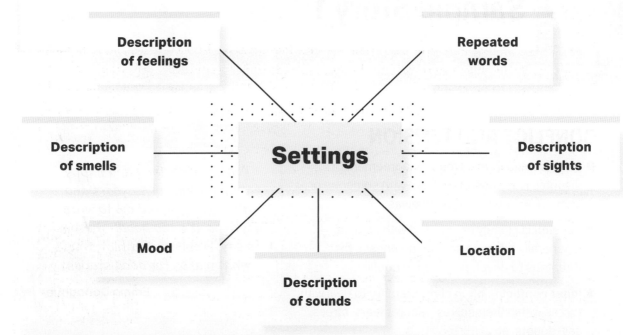

Description of feelings

Repeated words

Description of smells

Settings

Description of sights

Mood

Location

Description of sounds

NOTE

It's important to use the appropriate genre when writing. Leaving Cert short story titles are unlikely to expect mere narration throughout, but **the narrative element should play a significant part**. As with all compositions, you will be including language from several genres, such as description, information, etc.

SAMPLE SHORT STORY 1

Write a short story, set in a busy airport, in which a young security worker makes an important discovery. Your story may be menacing or amusing – or both.

MARKING SCHEME GUIDELINES

P: Focus on **a short story**, set in a busy airport, in which a young security worker makes an important discovery. The story may be menacing or amusing – or both.

Understanding of **genre**:
- the effective use of some elements of the short story, e.g. narrative shape, setting, plot, characterisation, suggestion, atmosphere, dialogue, tension, narrative voice, resolution, etc.

SAMPLE ANSWER

1. 'It's like a mini city out here!' said Femi, his wide face breaking into a happy grin. Jerry walked along behind the steady sound of Femi's quick steps. Why had he applied for this security job? 15 euro an hour, 40 hour week, health benefits, job security, no previous security experiance needed, full training provided. Yes, Jerry had it all carefully figured out. Unlike Femi who just always wanted to work at an airport. It didn't have to be Dublin. He loved the excitement of going away, of meeting different people from all over the world.

> Opening details establishes the airport setting and introduces characters.

2. He remembered the small air-conditioned classroom with its grey walls and low ceiling. For a week, 6 trainee security workers had listened to long lectures, learned how to deal with travellers, read x-ray images, practised pat-downs. The lecturer became very serious as he explained over and over how we were supposed to create a calm environment and show some authority to stop criminals and terrorists. Beads of sweat broke out on Jerry's forehead. It was soon to be the time for the first shift on the job.

> Good use of flashback. Close description of training adds realism.

3. The lecturer was still going, saying 'The security officer must perform each task as if their own lives and those of everyone around them were at stake!' At the busy checkpoint area in the airport, Jerry mouthed his learned script as he trailed behind the senior security officer to where passengers got their belongings checked. 'Empty all pockets, put your laptops and mobiles in the tray, remove your shoes, jackets and belts'. 'Right,' said the senior security officer, 'You're the person in charge.'

> Dialogue is effective in creating a build-up of tension in the security area.

4. Jerry's brand-new uniform, with its shiny name tag, felt a bit stiff uncomfortable. He didn't really feel in charge at all. He looked at the long lines of weary passengers. Remember, must keep the lines moving. The learned-off script swirled around in his head – phones, laptops, liquids, gels, aerosols, jackets. He watched the larger than life senior security officer in action. He brought a smile to the passengers' faces, even at 5 o'clock in the morning, with his loud performance of 'Show me the way to Amarillo.'

> Contrasting behaviour of the two characters highlight inexperience and confidence.

5. Jerry went over to two elderly passengers requesting pat-downs in order to avoid the scanner. One of them was in a wheel chair. 'I'll be using my hands to check the clothed areas of your body. I'll be clearing your around your and wasteline with my fingers.' The elderly man began to shake. The man shook his head. Suddenly Jerry's fingers felt a lump in the man's waistband. He curled his fingers round it and out popped a small plastic foil bag of cocaine.

6. 'Excuse me, sir, I'll have to ask you to accompany me to the security area on your right.' The man suddenly looked very pale and uneasy. 'She needs it for the pain.' Jerry's job was not to detain people, that was for the airport gardai. He spoke slowly into his walkie-talkie. The uniformed officers arrived quickly at the security clearance gate and took charge lf the situation.

> Although a lot happens very quickly in this dramatic scene, the storyline is developed reasonably well.

7. Jerry leaned against the marble wall. He was beginning to realise that beneath the surface glamour and buzz of an airport lay a frightening place where people didn't really matter. He began to wonder how many people are detained? How many have their belongings taken from them? He felt an interuption, an arm on his shoulder. Femi had reappeared. 'Alright mate?' Jerry, like the old man, just shook his head. 'You've done your job. Don't think about it anymore. You were told to leave all the stress at work.'

8. Jerry, hurryied through the crowds of passengers, pulling their cases and anxiously looking at their mobile phones and checking the timetable screens. He made his way outside to where the trees were rustling softly in the breeze. His breathing slowed as the affect of the gentle sounds relaxed him.

9. His future as a security officer appeared before him. Hour following hour of shift after shift of moving from one work station to the next, repeating the learnt script, studying everyone carefully and prying into their travel bags. Watching people hour after hour, catching them out. He still heard the lecturer's voice, 'Every pat down you do is to make sure the person in front of you is not a security risk'. He wondered what had become of the old man?

> Interesting take on Jerry's 'discovery' about the kind of work he wants to do.

10. Jerry shook his head. All his plans had come to nothing when faced with reality. His fingers pulled at his stiff collar. It was only a 6-month contract arrangment. He would quit the job. Next morning he went to the security company's office.

11. 'I want to resign,' he said to the girl at the desk.
Without even looking up at him for a second, she pushed two forms in front of him.
'Fill in your name, social security number and return the uniform immediately.'
She started typing again.
'Is that all?'
'Yeah, we're used to a high turnover.'

> Impressive final scene. Dialogue leaves readers thinking about the central character's experience.

(810 words)

NEW LANGUAGE LESSONS | COMPOSING

EXAMINER'S COMMENT

GRADE: H2

P = 26/30
C = 26/30
L = 25/30
M = 9/10

TOTAL = 86/100

- Focused well on a 'coming-of-age' workplace experience.
- A little more emphasis on the 'menacing' element expected.
- Interesting 'discoveries' about airport security work.
- Other notable features included setting, characterisation, dialogue and resolution.
- Effective use of revealing details and suggestion at the end, 'showing not telling'.
- Some mechanical errors ('experiance', 'wasteline', 'interuption', 'affect', 'arrangment').

CLASS/HOMEWORK ACTIVITY

Write the opening paragraph of a short story, set on a remote island off the west coast of Ireland, which features two young friends who discover a mysterious package washed up on the shore.

Aim for around 120 words.

PROMPT

- How does your opening scene establish the remote island setting?
- Are the two central characters swimming? Fishing? Or just walking along the beach?
- What does their conversation reveal? Are they relaxed? Bored? Looking for adventure?
- How will the opening paragraph suggest that something unexpected might happen?

Learning aim: To create credible fictional characters

CHARACTERISATION

- Characterisation refers to the **creation and development** of fictional characters.

- Writers present memorable characters through their physical **appearance and behaviour** – what the characters say, think, feel and do.

- Readers also learn about characters from the **reactions of other characters**.

- The author's direct **narrative voice** also reveals a character's personality.

- Leaving Cert short stories are generally around 800–850 words, leaving little time to fill in **a central character's history** or backstory.

- When writing a short story, **focus on a moment in the character's life that changes them**. Over the course of the story, they develop. They learn.

I try to create sympathy for my characters, then turn the monsters loose.

Stephen King

NOTE

Characters are **central to effective story-telling**. They keep the plot going and create human interest for readers to care about.

CHARACTER DESCRIPTION

Good story-tellers usually give readers just one or two **significant details** when portraying a character – for example, in this short description of a PE teacher:

> The legs were tucked into new white football socks, neatly folded at his ankles.

Does this portray a man who is fussy about his appearance? Is he also slightly ridiculous?

DESCRIPTION CAN BE DIRECT OR INDIRECT

In the following example, suggestion also gets readers thinking about a character:

> Cousin Kevin was always smiling. Not that any of us knew him very well. But I can't forget that afternoon when I happened to see him cruelly mistreating the family dog, From that moment on, I had second thoughts about him.

Instead of saying directly, *Kevin was hypocritical and brutal*, this short description is more interesting and involves readers in the character's secret life. As always, the best writing is suggestion: '**show, don't tell**'.

Body language (facial expressions and gestures) can also be revealing. Familiar mannerisms (habits), such as nervous fidgeting, clumsiness or vain hair-flicking can help to create a character.

A character's body language will often show their **mood or emotions**. Think about the different ways they might look and act when they are happy, confused, fearful, confident, etc.

STEREOTYPES

A stereotype is an exaggerated, **oversimplified character.** Stereotypes are sometimes referred to as **caricatures** – almost like cartoon figures. There is no depth to their personalities.

Stereotypes are one-dimensional and do not develop. They are often defined by **a single characteristic,** e.g. the clever scientist, the grumpy old man or the rebellious teenager.

Stereotyping can be both misleading and sometimes offensive. **Short story-writing offers you an opportunity to be imaginative** in creating realistic characters who have more depth. The well-rounded character will even surprise the reader.

> **NOTE**
>
> In real life, few people are entirely good or bad. Most have **more than one side to their personality**. Keep this in mind when creating credible characters.

HOW CHARACTERS SPEAK

The **use of dialogue is important in narrative writing.** It can reveal character and speed up the story. It's sometimes effective to start with a conversation or argument between two characters. This could introduce tension or conflict. It can also provide backstory.

No two people are ever exactly the same. Not only in their appearance, but in the way they speak. Individuals will use language in a way that **reveals their personality**. They will have expressions and favourite slang: *Ah, sure look … It was just awesome! Like, you know … OK Stop!*

Creating different voices which sound authentic will show the examiner your narrative writing skills. **Characters come to life** through speaking in dialogue.

FORESHADOWING

Foreshadowing hints at where the story is going. Like a game of cat and mouse, the writer teases the reader about developments and plot turns that may occur later in the story.

This creates an **atmosphere of suspense** and adds dramatic tension by building up expectations. It also makes extraordinary events believable because readers have been prepared in advance for them.

Readers can sometimes become unhappy and frustrated if their curiosity has been excited by foreshadowing that then leads nowhere. An exception to this, of course, is in mystery or crime stories where the author deliberately sets up false leads (known as 'red herrings').

SAMPLE SHORT STORY 2

Write a short story which starts with an argument between a shop assistant and a dissatisfied customer, and eventually leads to shocking consequences.

MARKING SCHEME GUIDELINES

P: Focus on **a short story** which starts with an argument between a shop assistant and a dissatisfied customer, and eventually leads to shocking consequences.

Understanding of **genre**:
- the effective use of some elements of the short story, e.g. narrative shape, setting, plot, characterisation, suggestion, atmosphere, dialogue, tension, narrative voice, resolution, etc.

SAMPLE ANSWER

1. All the trouble began in a chemist shop. 'I want to make a complaint,' the hoodied young teen said to the smart shop assistant. 'We don't take complaints at the counter. You have to email your complaint in to our company's complaint section.' This definately angered the teen. 'I am making a serious complaint to you because you sold me this product under totally false pretences,' said the young teen back. But the assistant just repeated, 'Just stand back and allow the other customers to be served. You can Email your complaint into the complaint department of our company.'

> Opening establishes the conflict. A few details would make both the setting and characters more authentic.

2. 'I will not. You sold me this hair product which does not do what you said on the cover that it would do. So you are the one I am complaining to.' The annoying girl behind the cash counter was now getting really angry as well. 'If you stay here and make a scene with me, I am going to call security.'

3. Suddenly the hoodied teen found herself lifted by two strong security staff officers and carried on to the pavement just outside the chemist shop. 'You are now banned from entering the store ever again,' said one of the two top security guards. The teen just sat there in total disbelief and shock. How had the whole thing come to this?

4. A week ago, she had entered the chemist shop in a very happy mood. She was going to buy hair dye for the end of the school year graduation dance. She was really looking forward to it. The whole gang would be there. It was going to be a fantastic night, just before they were to split up to go their different ways now that school had ended.

> Brief flashback is a good attempt at developing the main character's personality.

5. She had gone straight up to the smart shop assistant and spoken to her. 'I would like to buy Scharz Brights in shocking pink, please'. The smart shop girl looked at the teen with total pity. 'That is just so unfashionable,' she smirked. 'Everyone these days is buying Punkii Colour in bright magenta. It's the latest hair colouring and it's totally 100% cruelty free.'

Expression lacks control and is repetitive – 'just' and 'totally' over-used.

6. The young teen was really interested. 'The 100% cruelty free sounds good,' she said. Her class had just had a talk from Petta about the suffering of animals in lab experiment on cosmetics. 'OK so then,' said the teen. 'I'll take Punkii Colour'. 'It's really very good,' said the assistant. 'So you will be completly delighted with the result. I can promise you that.'

7. The teen went straight home. That night she applied Punkii Colour. It felt different from the usual cream she used but it was cruelty free. She would leave it on for the twenty minutes as it said on the instruction leaflet. After ten minutes or so she felt her whole scalp starting to tingle. Then she felt it get very hot. She put her head under the shower to rinse the cream off. Suddenly she noticed handfuls of purple hair all over the shower tray. 'Oh God,' she cried. 'I'm going completly bald.' Soon enough, she was as bald as an egg.

8. Well, that was the final turning point. The next day she went right back to the chemist shop first thing in the morning. She would of gone a lot sooner but wasn't sure what she should do but she would definately do something. Sitting on the ground, outside the store, the young teen had a total brain wave. She pulled a piece of cardboard from the rubbish bin. Then using a big red marker, she wrote 'Go into this chemist shop and you will become totally bald.' She pulled off her hoodie and sat on it, her bald patches were there on show for all to see.

Plot builds effectively to a climax through paragraphs 7 and 8.

9. A big crowd gathered. The young reporter for the local newspaper interviewed her. The young teen also posted her personal story on social media. It soon went totally viral. People passing and shoppers started stopping to ask her about what happened. Nobody past her protest. For two weeks nobody at all went into the chemist.

List of events is unrealistic. Expression is also awkward.

10. Finally, on the second Friday, the smart assistant came out with red eyes. She was crying and clutching an envelope in her hand. 'It's all thanks to you, I got fired,' she said. The young teen smiled. For once in her life, this was a proper victory for her. It felt better than emailing the complaints department.

The story is well rounded off, leaving readers to make up their own minds about the central character.

(740 words)

GRADE: H3

P =   22/30
C =   21/30
L =   19/30
M =   9/10

TOTAL = 71/100

- This short response takes on the task in the title to shape a modern-day revenge story.

- Narrative features are reasonably well handled, e.g. setting, conflict and plot development.

- Storyline is engaging, but vague and unconvincing at times (e.g. paragraph 9).

- Dialogue would have been more effective if laid out in paragraphs.

- Language use is repetitive and expression is awkward occasionally.

- Some mechanical errors ('e.g. 'definately', 'Petta', 'completly', 'of gone', 'past').

CLASS/HOMEWORK ACTIVITY

Write a paragraph describing a moment of conflict or tension for inclusion in a short story about a well-meaning character who gets into unexpected trouble for telling the truth.

Aim for around 120 words.

PROMPT

- Does miscommunication create tension in this dramatic scene?
- Is the conflict obvious? Or is the tension simmering beneath the surface?
- Any sense of the situation becoming even more intense and angry?
- Does the writing and dialogue 'show' rather than 'tell'?

Learning aim: To analyse science fiction features in a sample story

- Science fiction (or futuristic fiction) is a genre of literature which usually includes **imagined elements** that don't exist in the real world.

- **Sci-fi explores many subjects,** particularly advances in technology and science. Stories are often set in the future and readers are presented with unfamiliar universes, such as outer space, alien life, inner earth, robots and time travel.

- **Dystopian science fiction** presents disturbing visions of oppressive societies.

- Ordinary people usually play an important part in sci-fi narratives even though the stories are often very **critical of the human race's failings.**

> **NOTE**
>
> How humans interact with science and technology is central to science fiction.

WRITING GOOD SCIENCE FICTION

To write a believable sci-fi story, you have to **create a new world** instead of relying on familiar settings and societies. Strange planets and parallel universes to our own are likely locations.

It's best to set your story in the **not-too-distant future** where you can create machines and cities that looks like advanced versions of what we already know.

Be careful about including monsters and magic – both belong more in fantasy stories.

Take time to **plan** the plot (storyline):

- What **key point** do you want to make about **human beings** and their **impact** on the world?

- What **changes** will happen over the course of your story?

- What will your central character **learn**?

SHAPING YOUR STORY

- A **strong opening** will make readers want to know more.
- Choose a **narrative point of view**. Who is telling the story?
- Establish **setting and central characters** early on.
- Then **move on to the conflict** and get straight into the action.
- Avoid having **too many** characters.
- Keep the plot **simple.**
- **Dialogue** can often heighten the drama.
- **Build up the story** to a climax or turning point.
- The **ending** should be memorable, although not necessarily happy-ever-after.

CLASS/HOMEWORK ACTIVITY

Opening sentences have to hook readers into the story and establish the tone. Sci-fi openings need to introduce in a whole new alternative world.

From the three examples shown here, choose the opening sentence that you think is most effective in drawing you into the story. Briefly explain your choice.

(Aim for around 120 words.)

1 'The last man on Earth sat alone in a room. There was a knock on the door.'
Fredric Brown
Wonder Stories

2 'Once upon a time, there was a Martian named Valentine Michael Smith.'
Robert A. Heinlein
Stranger in a Strange Land

3 'Let's start with the end of the world, why don't we?'
N.K. Jemisin
The Fifth Season

SAMPLE ANSWER

Number 3 is the best example as it gets me into thinking of how the world actually did end. Obviously, in a science fiction story, there's a chance of an alien invasion. So this would be interesting. Of course, another planet could have crashed into the earth or possibly it was a future nuclear war or some natural disaster. Everyone would have their own ideas for sure as to how life as we know it ended. In my opinion, this is the most imaginative first sentence because it starts me wondering. I think most people would have their own views on what went wrong. If you think about it, what could be a bigger thing than the end of the world?

EXAMINER'S COMMENT

- Solid high-grade response, giving some good reasons for choosing the third opening.
- Insightful focus on the wide range of likely reactions from readers.
- Expression is clear, overall, but slightly repetitive ('own ideas', 'own views').

USING DIALOGUE EFFECTIVELY

1. Use a capital letter to begin the sentence

Put inverted commas around what the character says.

Place commas, full stops, exclamation and question marks that refer to the direct speech inside the inverted commas.

- 'See you soon', said Mary. ✘
- 'See you soon,' said Mary. ✔

2. Take a new line for each change of speaker.

- 'I wish the Leaving Cert was over,' Deirdre sighed. 'Don't wish your life away,' Dad replied. ✘
- 'I wish the Leaving Cert. was over,' Deirdre sighed.
  'Don't wish your life away,' Dad replied. ✔

3. Break up a long line of dialogue when it helps readers know who is speaking.

- 'I just don't believe I've failed. I studied and studied, but I just went blank … I think I'm going to have to re-sit,' said Niall. ✘
- 'I just don't believe I've failed,' said Niall. 'I studied and studied, but I just went blank … I think I'm going to have to re-sit.' ✔

4. If only two people are speaking, once you have established who they are, you can drop the dialogue verbs altogether.

- 'You have broken my heart,' she sobbed.
  'Don't blame me he muttered.
  'You cheated on me!' she screamed.
  'I don't know – it just happened,' he mumbled.
  'Oooh!' she cried. ✘
- 'You have broken my heart,' she sobbed.
  'Don't blame me,' he said.
  'You cheated on me!'
  'I don't know – it just happened.'
  'Oooh!' ✔

NOTE

Some writers dispense with the usual rules for dialogue, often just using a new line with no punctuation marks to indicate speech. For the Leaving Certificate examination, however, it's best to use the **formal rules for dialogue.**

CLASS/HOMEWORK ACTIVITY

Rewrite the following passage using the guidelines for dialogue above to make the story clearer for the reader.

Do you see that? She dumped a fresh pot of coffee in the sink. Yeah, I replied, pointing to the steam. Woman in booth 51 thinks the coffee's too cold. Lyn grimaced. Sharing her frustration, I offered my advice. Maybe you should accidentally spill a little drop of it on her, so she'll really know how hot it is. We giggled secretly, half-wishing it was an option. I watched Lyn take the rest of the lady's order as I retreated into booth 60, just across from 51, my cup of coffee blowing fragrant steam at my face. Ooops! cried Lyn as the hot brown liquid trickled onto the lady's table. We exchanged glances and Lyn winked.

(See corrected version on page 177)

SAMPLE SHORT STORY 3

Write a short story, to be included in a new Science Fiction collection, set in 2050 when Planet Earth is completely enveloped in unexplained darkness.

MARKING SCHEME GUIDELINES

P: Focus on **a short story** for a new Science Fiction collection, set in 2050 when Planet Earth is completely enveloped in unexplained darkness.

Understanding of **genre**:

● the effective use of some elements of the sci-fi short story genre, e.g. narrative shape, setting, plot, characterisation, suggestion, atmosphere, dialogue, tension, narrative voice, resolution, etc.

SAMPLE ANSWER

1. 'Peep, peep!' The old-fashioned alarm clock croaked. Toby rubbed his eyes. He stared sleepily at the retro battery clock. 8am! He flipped open his super-iPhone – blank black screen. Had he forgotten to charge it? Toby jumped out of bed, clicking on the bedside lamp. Nothing! He slipped on his tracksuit and runners and yanked back the bedroom curtains. Total blackness stared back at him.

> Opening invites readers into a futuristic setting and the odd darkness.

2. Toby skipped lightly downstairs, flicking light switches as he went. Still nothing! He opened the creaky front door – inky blackness enveloped him. Not a single street light to be seen. Not a star in the sky. Toby ran his hands through his hair. What was this? Surely, they hadn't finally done it? For several months, at the Earth Summit Meetings, there had been non-stop planning and threats. Global warming had now become global boiling.

> Develops storyline by introducing a possible reason for the unusual events.

3. He slipped his fingers into the space beside the front door. It was still there. His grandfather's words came into Toby's head, 'You never know when you might need it!' Toby curled his fingers around the thin cylinder of the old battery torch and pulled it out. He squeezed the button. It worked! A small light at last in the inky night. Toby smiled to himself, imagine it still worked in 2050! He carefully made his way down the old path. An eerie silence surrounded him. No cars sped past him. He crossed the road to Mrs. Murphy's house. He heard a slight creak. He pointed his torch. Toby called out, 'Anyone in?' No voice answered. Toby froze beside the garden wall. They had done it. They said they would. He tapped his forehead. Think! Think! His head sank into his hands.

> Good attempt at building up tension.

4. Meanwhile In the large oval summit room, the Leader was speaking to his closest advisers. He was discussing the idea of spraying dust particles into the sun to block out its hot rays. One of the scientists rose slowly to her feet. 'But our whole planet is based on chlorophyll, the plants need the sun's rays to grow.' Her voice echoed in the large summit room. The Leader

> Cinematic scene links conflict to climate action.

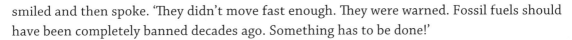

smiled and then spoke. 'They didn't move fast enough. They were warned. Fossil fuels should have been completely banned decades ago. Something has to be done!'

5. Back in the inky dark night, Toby got up. There has to be someone, somewhere. The light stretched out in front of him. He began to run. The only sound was the quick pant of his breath as he sprinted along the dark road. Open front doors flapped under the golden light of his torch. Out of breath, Toby sank onto the grass. He flipped off his torch. Tears pricked his eyes.

6. The movement had started out with such good intentions. They really believed they were saving the planet. He remembered the day he and his girlfriend had joined in the protest at the President's home. Giggling and laughing, they had arrived in their bright orange gear, hauling ladders and large rolls of inky black material. They had climbed up onto the roof of the President's home, unfurling the rolls of black material. The house was now destroyed under the cover of black inky darkness. They had got good coverage on the media to highlight the President's decision to stop granting oil and gas licenses. They both agreed it was important to keep raising awareness.

> Details add some interesting backstory.

7. Toby suddenly felt a warm furry presence beside him. He flipped on the torch again. A large golden retriever sat beside him. A sloppy wet lick was placed on Toby's arm. Two brown eyes gazed into his. Toby patted the gentle dog. 'Good boy, good boy! Looks like it's just you and me!' Suddenly the dog stretched and began to pad along the road.

8. The dog began to pick up pace. Toby followed. He flicked on the torch again. The dog slipped through the gate and began to run along the rough track which weaved between the fields. Toby followed. The dog ran to the old cave at the mountain base and stopped. Toby caught up.

9. He shone his torch into the cave and followed the dog who disappeared behind a jutting piece of rock. Toby ducked around it. He suddenly found himself surrounded by shining golden beams of light. The golden retriever shape suddenly shifted into one of the most stunning light beams – and then it seemed to begin to speak.

10. 'Welcome to the Fifth Dimension. You are the last Earthling to be rescued from dying Mother Earth. You will soon be programmed and taken up to the next reality to join the others. We Light Beings will finally solve Mother Earth's problems. She needs light to live and clean air to breathe. Although his intentions are good, Man is on the wrong path. When all the damage is corrected, we will return you!'

11. Toby started to feel weightless and he began to rise through one of the beams of light. He felt a great sense of peace as he rose upwards.

> Strong build-up to the dramatic ending.
>
> Final scenes highlight the story's 'message'.

(830 words)

EXAMINER'S COMMENT

GRADE: H1
P = 28/30
C = 27/30
L = 25/30
M = 10/10
TOTAL = 90/100

- Imaginative story based on a character facing an extraordinary situation.
- Good attempt at including some futuristic sci-fi features.
- The many references to light and darkness are in keeping with the title.
- Details, such as the clock and torch, help establish setting.
- Storyline is well organised into scenes which build to a highpoint.
- Expression could be more varied (e.g. 'inky' is over-used) and there is some awkward repetition in paragraphs 6 and 8.

ENDGAME

There is **no single right or wrong approach to ending a short story**, but most writers usually know how the narrative will end before they begin, and so they can focus on the resolution as they are writing.

The ending should leave readers satisfied that it is **credible within the 'world' of the story** and it must be true to its characters. A successful conclusion solves the central conflict. This can be done happily or unhappily (or a mix of both).

> People die, love dies, but life does not die, and so long as people live, stories must have life at the end.
>
> **John O'Hara**

The writer can provide a **twist in the tale** when readers will be surprised or even shocked by the outcome, but the ending must not seem out of place in the story.

The ending can be **closed**, so that nothing more can happen and there are no unanswered questions.

If the story is **open-ended** (a cliff-hanger), readers are left to come up with their own ideas about what happened.

Think carefully about **the tone** of your ending. Do you want it to be happy? Sad? Funny?

Readers will usually expect the conclusion to **tie up the loose ends in a convincing way** and answer any questions that have arisen over the course of the story.

EFFECTIVE CONCLUSIONS

- Resolve the main conflict in **a credible way**.
- Circular plots where the **ending echoes the opening** create a sense of finality.
- A cliff-hanger ending leaves readers to decide what is likely to happen next.
- Memorable **endings can be touching and thought-provoking**. If the conclusion is unrealistic or too neat, it can weaken the story.
- The ending should **make an impact.** Something should have been learned about human nature and behaviour – without being preachy.

NOTE

It's best to avoid clichéd or unconvincing endings, such as:

- *Lucky for me, all my problems were solved when I unexpectedly won millions on the Lotto.*

- *It was really my evil twin, you see. We were separated at birth.*

- *Actually, I'm really a cat/ghost/alien.*

- *Guess what? It had all been a terrible dream …*

CLASS/HOMEWORK ACTIVITY

Write the concluding paragraph for a short story in which you play key role in helping your local Gardaí solve a mystery.

Aim for around 120 words.

PROMPT

- Where does the final scene take place? Is the setting significant?

- Do readers know what the central character is thinking or feeling? Does it seem that the characters have learned a valuable lesson?

- How have they changed? What have they lost or gained?

- Is the final mood positive or negative?

CORRECTED CLASS/HOMEWORK ACTIVITY

(See page 173)

'Do you see that?'

She dumped a fresh pot of coffee in the sink.

'Yeah,' I replied, pointing to the steam. 'Woman in booth 51 thinks the coffee's too cold.'

Lyn grimaced. Sharing her frustration, I offered my advice.

'Maybe you should accidentally spill a little drop of it on her, so she'll really know how hot it is.'

We giggled secretly, half-wishing it was an option. I watched Lyn take the rest of the lady's order as I retreated into booth 60, just across from 51, my cup of coffee blowing fragrant steam at my face.

'Ooops!' cried Lyn as the hot brown liquid trickled onto the lady's table.

We exchanged glances and Lyn winked.

SAMPLE COMPOSING QUESTIONS

Write a composition on any one of the assignments below.

Each composition carries 100 marks.

The composition assignments are intended to reflect language study in the areas of information, argument, persuasion, narration and the aesthetic use of language.

(Aim for around 850–900 words over 80 minutes.)

1. Write a reflective personal essay on the significance of family and friends in your life.
2. Write a descriptive essay about a particular place (or places) that have a special significance for you.
3. Write a short story in which a close friendship between two students suddenly changes when one of them decides to end the friendship for no apparent reason.
4. Write a discursive feature article about the value and relevance of studying Shakespeare's plays in today's world.
5. Write an informative article for a popular online magazine aimed at young adults, giving them advice about making the most of life after the Leaving Cert.
6. Write a personal essay in which you reflect on what you believe are the most important achievements in your life.
7. Write a short story (serious or light-hearted) which features a rebellious teenager who suddenly becomes front page news.

NOTE

Examiners remarked positively on some candidates' skills in crafting memorable short stories. These candidates displayed confidence in their handling of elements of short story writing such as: narrative shape; effective characterisation; developing a coherent plot; attention to aspects of setting (including time, period and place); the use of dialogue and the creation of atmosphere (including the skilful use of drama and tension). Short stories are more effective when the readers are drawn into the story through the effective use of suggestion and a well-controlled narrative structure.

Source: Chief Examiner's Report
(www.examinations.ie)

LESSON 40 Mechanics – Grammar and Spelling

Learning aim: To revise essential grammar and spelling for Leaving Cert English

MECHANICS

Marks awarded for **Accuracy of Mechanics (M)** refer to spelling and grammar, appropriate to the register.

Marks for **M** are essentially **independent** of Purpose (P), Coherence (C) and Language (L) marks.

Correct grammar is essential for clarity and understanding. It can be defined in various ways:

● The **structure of sentences**, including syntax (word order).

● The **basic language rules** about usage of Standard English that is widely regarded as correct and acceptable.

Word Class	Function	Example
Nouns	'naming words'	Limerick, lunch, happiness, group
Verbs	'doing words'	imagine, sing, comprehend, defy
Adjectives	'describing words'	enormous, critical, wry, positive
Adverbs	mainly describe verbs	incredibly, most, really, quite
Pronouns	take the place of nouns	I, she, him, me, their, it, our
Connectives	'joining words'	and, or, if, but, so, because, yet
Prepositions	provide information about time and place	since, before, until, through, next to

SOME COMMONLY MISUSED WORDS

Homophones are words that sound the same but are spelt differently. They also have different meanings, e.g. break and brake; to, two and too.

If you are unsure about the correct spelling of a particular word, check it in a dictionary.

FREQUENTLY MISUSED WORDS

The following words are often confused:

Accept: verb meaning to 'agree' or to 'receive' something.
Except: preposition meaning 'with the exclusion of'.

E.g.   *I would like you to **accept** this small gift.*
      *All my friends came to the party – **except** for Kate.*

Advice: noun meaning an opinion or guidance.
Advise: verb meaning to 'counsel' or make a suggestion.

E.g.   *Declan gave me some good **advice** about our noisy neighbours.*
      *I also asked Clóna to **advise** me about them.*

Affect: verb meaning to 'influence'.
Effect: noun meaning the 'result of an action'.

E.g.   *Poor grammar may **affect** your marks.*
      *Poor grammar had a huge **effect** on Leo's results.*

Allowed: past participle of the verb 'to allow', meaning 'permitted'.
Aloud: adjective, meaning 'out loud'.

E.g.   *The children are not **allowed** to go to the cinema this evening.*
      *Ronan was asked to read the poem **aloud**.*

Have: verb meaning possess; also used as an auxiliary (support) verb
Of: preposition used in phrases.

E.g.   *Shane could **have** played for Leinster.*
      *Don watches lots **of** sport on TV.*

Its: meaning 'belong to it'.
It's: short for 'it is'.

E.g.   *Sara's cat keeps licking **its** paw.*
      ***It's** time for our class to go to the gym.*

Less: usually describes single items.
Fewer: refers to people or things in the plural.

E.g.   *My friend is spending **less** time with me these days.*
      *We might have **fewer** arguments if I wasn't so difficult.*

Loose: adjective meaning 'not fastened or restrained'.
Lose: verb, has many meanings such as to 'not win' or to 'mislay'.

E.g.   *That roof tile is **loose** and might fall at any minute.*
      *Let's hope we don't **lose** the big match on Saturday.*

Passed: verb – the past tense of the verb to 'pass'.
Past: noun and adjective referring to the time before the present.

E.g.   *Ben **passed** the ball to the striker.*
      *Lucy hoped that the misunderstanding was now in the **past**.*
      *The **past** week has been busy.*

Look for the bare necessities ... or are they bear necessities?

Practise: verb meaning to 'prepare'.
Practice: noun meaning 'preparation'.

E.g. *Emily **practised** her lines for the school play.*
*It takes a lot of **practice** to become fluent in Irish.*

Principal: adjective and noun, meaning most important or chief.
Principle: noun meaning 'value or belief'.

E.g. *Paris is France's **principal** city.*
*The **principle** of free speech should never be taken for granted.*
*The children were excited about meeting the new school **principal**.*

Quite: adverb, means 'not completely'.
Quiet: adjective, means 'not noisy'.

E.g. *The students are exceptionally **quiet** today ... Spooky or what?*
*I've been **quite** busy all day. I hope things ease up soon.*

Stationary: adjective, meaning 'not moving'.
Stationery: noun, meaning 'office supplies'.

E.g. *The bus remained **stationary** until the lights turned green.*
*Our school secretary is in charge of ordering **stationery**.*

Their: possessive pronoun meaning 'belonging to them'.
There: adverb commonly used to mean 'in that place'.
There is also used at the beginning of sentences.
They're: short for 'they are'.

E.g. *The neighbours are away again, so I have to feed **their** three cats.*
*They live over **there** beside the pet shop..*
***There** are two of the cats that never stop hissing at me.*
***They're** going to be a challenge over the next week.*

WHICH WITCH IS WHICH?

To: preposition often used with a verb.
Too: adverb meaning 'extremely' or 'also'.
Two: refers to the number 2.

E.g. *My sister drives **to** work every day.*
*I'm just **too** tired to watch TV.*
***Two** little children were playing on the swings.*

Whether: used in indirect questions to introduce one alternative.
Weather: noun meaning the 'state of the atmosphere.'

E.g. *I'm not sure **whether** Sheena is from Balbriggan or Blackrock.*
*I hope the **weather** is going to be fantastic tomorrow.*

Your: pronoun meaning 'belonging to you'.
You're: short for 'you are'.

E.g. ***Your** dad's van is blocking our drive again.*
*It looks like **you're** going nowhere.*

USE THE RIGHT PHRASE!

- 'a lot' means 'many' and should be written as two separate words.
- 'as well' is also written as two words.
- 'may be' usually means 'might be'.
- 'maybe' means 'perhaps'.
- 'no one' is a two-word phrase.
- 'nobody' is one word.
- 'thank you' is always written as two words.

IMPROVING LEAVING CERTIFICATE ANSWERS

Your written responses must always be carefully planned and organised. Decide on the main points that you wish to make. You can write your response using paragraphs.

PARAGRAPH ALERT!

A paragraph is a section of text, usually consisting of a group of sentences, which addresses a particular topic or aspect of a subject.

Paragraphs can be any length, but as a general guide, it will take at least three or four sentences to make a point and develop it with reference or commentary.

A paragraph may occasionally be one sentence (or even one word) for a particular effect.

WHAT IS A PARAGRAPH?

Paragraphs have been compared to signposts for readers. New paragraphs indicate a change of focus, e.g. a different argument, a new setting, etc.

WHY USE PARAGRAPHS?

- Paragraphs break up long texts and give structure to a piece of writing. They help to organise your thoughts and clarify your ideas.
- Every paragraph should discuss just one main idea, so that the examiner is able to identify what it is about.
- Paragraphs are usually based around a topic sentence – **a key statement which is expanded in the rest of the paragraph. The topic sentence (which is often at the start or end of the paragraph) is central to the point you are making and should relate back to the exam question.**

Identify the topic sentence in each of the following paragraphs and comment briefly on how the central idea is developed within the rest of the paragraph.

The first one is done for you.

SAMPLE PARAGRAPH 1

More emphasis on truth is also needed in the business world. Big businesses employ smart lawyers to find loopholes in the law to avoid paying taxes and to find ways around planning restrictions. Advertising agencies fill the potential customers with fear or impossible dreams in order to convince them to buy. The truth is often, unlike the profits, in short supply. 'You will get bad skin if you do not use our product,' they threaten. 'You will always look young if you use our product,' they promise.

SAMPLE ANSWER

I think that the topic sentence is 'More emphasis on truth is also needed in the business world'. What then follows in the rest of the paragraph gives a number of very good examples of the lack of honesty in big business today, such as when they employ 'smart lawyers' or fool customers with threats and flattery. The idea of using advertising quotes is really effective and emphasises the central point that profits are what matters most in business and that the truth is 'in short supply'.

SAMPLE PARAGRAPH 2

Medical research has significantly lengthened our lives with new medicines and treatments such as laser surgery. Early diagnosis is now the key to prevention as well as cure. There is no limit to the possibilities for science and technology in the future. We are waiting on the day when cancer is also a curable disease like polio and leprosy. We are now able to offer laser eye treatment to people to restore twenty/twenty vision.

SAMPLE PARAGRAPH 3

In the dark arena a flash of silver gleams as the harsh tuning of the orchestra continues. The sound engineers with their familiar 'testing-one-two-one-two' finish checking the stage microphones. The percussion players march on stage. Applause ripples from the audience as the conductor enters. A moment's pause as the slim white baton rises, the audience holds its breath and the warm opening notes of 'The Mikado Overture' transport all to the world of Japan. This is the magic of live performance.

> **NOTE**
>
> The main aim is to **use paragraphs appropriately** – and this will depend on the actual question, the time available, and, of course, the language genre.

WHEN DO I START A NEW PARAGRAPH?

Start a new paragraph for each new point or stage in your writing. Be aware of the main idea being expressed in your paragraph and how clear it is for your reader.

In all hand-written answers, either indent or skip a line for new paragraphs.

PARAGRAPH PROBLEMS

- The central idea or key point isn't clear.
- Poorly organised, hard to follow.
- Note-like list of separate sentences.
- Too many ideas in one paragraph.
- No sense of developing the central idea.

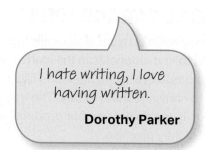

I hate writing, I love having written.

Dorothy Parker

CLASS/HOMEWORK REVISION ACTIVITIES

1. **Rewrite this passage, correcting the five spelling errors:**

   Jenny is my best freind, but she can be quiet wierd at times. In fact, she's begining to get on my nerves about all the celibritys she keeps mentioning.

2. **Rewrite the following, selecting the correct options:**

   I really want my sister to get her driving license/licence so that she can drive me to football practise/ practice every second night. I've adviced/advised her to practise/practice as much as possible.

3. **Rewrite the following sentences so that they make sense:**

   (a) Did you notice those monkeys over their at the cars?

   (b) They've actually taken there windscreen wipers.

   (c) There so cute.

   (d) I think their now hiding just over they're.

4. **Rewrite the following, selecting the correct options:**

   (a) The Finance Ministers'/Minister's spokesperson was not impressed.

   (b) Jim threw the men's/mens' boots into the bin.

   (c) The student's/students' noses all turned blue in the cold.

   (d) The baby's/babys' cot is really cute.

5. **Rewrite the following sentences so that they make sense:**

   (a) Who's/Whose going to the party?

   (b) Who's/Whose bag is this?

6. **Rewrite each of these sentences correctly:**

   (a) Such inmature and inconsiderate behaviour fills me with unbelief.

   (b) Misfortunately, we were inaware that the ticket was unvalid.

   (c) It was disbelievable that the writing was so unlegible.

   (d) Some of the rules were completely unrelevant.

7. **Rewrite the following, selecting the correct options:**

   (a) How does eating too much chocolate effect/affect your blood sugar?

   (b) We should of/have brought hats and umbrellas with us.

   (c) The principle/principal ingredients of bread are flour, water and yeast.

   (d) Dee will not be able to accept/except the new job offer.

   (e) The button on my sleeve is (loose, lose) and if I (loose, lose) that button, I'm in deep trouble.

8. **Rewrite correctly:**

   Cillian worried that he wasn't getting alot of sleep.

9. **Rewrite the following, correcting all errors:**

   the great american writer mark twain once said when i was a boy of 14 my father was so ignorant i could hardly stand to have the old man around of course when i got to be 21 I was astonished at how much the old man had learned in seven years

10. **Rewrite the following, adding all necessary punctuation and speech marks:**

    Have you found the advanced philosophy course interesting and fruitful, my dear he asked. His tone indicated that he was a little fearful she might say no. He peered over his half-glasses. Oh Dr Morgan how could it be otherwise, when we have the benefit of such an amazingly awesome mind like yours applying itself to the greatest, most profound, issues of the human condition? Yes indeed I'm glad you noticed that he intoned. Not to mention that you're such a totally charming gentleman. Ciara batted her eyes at him, sending a shower of mascara down his eye-catching lurid pink tie. Charming is good … Keep talking Morgan mumbled as he stuffed one of the ridiculously small sandwiches into his mouth

[Answers overleaf]

Chief Examiner's Report

Candidates who displayed a capacity to communicate fluently and effectively were rewarded. However, the management and control of language continues to pose problems for some candidates and, in particular, poor attention to the formal aspects of language, such as spelling, grammar and punctuation, was noted in some responses.

(www.examinations.ie)

(pages 184–185)

1. Jenny is my best **friend**, but she can be **quite weird** at times. In fact, she's **beginning** to get on my nerves about all the **celebrities** she keeps mentioning.

2. I really want my sister to get her driving **licence** so that she can drive me to football **practice** every second night. I've advised her to **practise** as much as possible.

3. (a) Did you notice those monkeys over **there** at the cars?

   (b) They've actually taken **their** windscreen wipers.

   (c) **They're** so cute.

   (d) I think **they're** now hiding just over **there**.

4. (a) The Finance **Minister's** spokesperson was not impressed.

   (b) Jim threw the **men's** boots into the bin.

   (c) The **students'** noses all turned blue in the cold.

   (d) The **baby's** cot is really cute.

5. (a) **Who's** going to the party?

   (b) **Whose** bag is this?

6. (a) Such immature and inconsiderate behaviour fills me with **disbelief**.

   (b) **Unfortunately**, we were unaware that the ticket was invalid.

   (c) It was **unbelievable** that the writing was so illegible.

   (d) Some of the rules were completely **irrelevant**.

7. (a) How does eating too much chocolate affect your blood sugar?

   (b) We should **have** brought hats and umbrellas with us.

   (c) The **principal** ingredients of bread are flour, water and yeast.

   (d) Dee will not be able to a**ccept** the new job offer.

   (e) The button on my sleeve is **loose** and if I **lose** that button, I'm in deep trouble.

8. Cillian worried that he wasn't getting **a lot** of sleep.

9. The great **American** writer **Mark Twain** once said: '**When I** was a boy of 14, my father was so ignorant I could hardly stand to have the old man around. **Of course,** when I got to be **21,** I was astonished at how much the old man had learned in seven years.'

10. 'Have you found the advanced philosophy course interesting, my dear?' he asked. His tone indicated that he was a little fearful she might say no. He peered over his half-glasses.

    'Oh, Dr Morgan, how could it be otherwise, when we have the benefit of such an amazingly awesome mind like yours applying itself to the greatest, most profound, issues of the human condition?'

    'Yes, indeed, I'm glad you noticed that,' he intoned.

    'Not to mention that you're such a totally charming gentleman.' Ciara batted her eyes at him, sending a shower of mascara down his eye-catching lurid pink tie.

    'Charming is good … Keep talking,' Morgan mumbled, as he stuffed one of the ridiculously small sandwiches into his mouth.